CW00499999

THE THICK RED LINE

(One story of the British Army)

by

Ian Patterson

Acknowledgements

I would like to thank my son John, who spent 17 years in the Royal Engineers. This collection of stories was inspired by his humerous anecdotes told to me during his service career. Many of them are based upon John's own personal experiences and those of his comrades-in-arms.

In addition, thanks to Bill Hall in Australia, ex-engineer; Dennis Powell, ex-Herefordshire's; Billy Heslop, ex-signals, Doug Hewer, Royal Welsh Fusiliers and Harry Wright, ex-King's Own Yorkshire Light Infantry, for their input.

*****

"But it's Thin red line of 'eroes' when the drums begin to roll -
The drums begin to roll, my boys, the drums begin to roll,
O it's the Thin red line of 'eroes' when the drums begin to roll."

Rudyard Kipling

*****

Any similarity to any person, living or dead; is purely coincidental.

Copyright © James Ian Patterson and John Adam Patterson 2007

The rights of James Ian Patterson to be identified as the writer of this work
have been asserted in accordance with the Copyright Designs and Patents Act 1988.

No part of this publication may be reproduced in any form or by
means, graphic, electronic, or mechanical, including photocopying, recording, taping
or information storage and retrieval systems - without the prior written permission of
the publisher.

Published by GET Publishing, 57 Queens Road, Bridgnorth, Shropshire WV15 5DG
info@getpublishing.co.uk

ISBN 978-0-9556464-3-0

Printed in the United Kingdom by Direct Imagery Limited, 3 Prince Road, Kings Norton, Birmingham B30 3HB

The stories in this book do contain a certain amount of 'black humour' so prevalent amongst all the services, whether police or military, and we make no apology for that. It is a necessary part of the way in which ordinary people deal with the exceptional circumstances they find themselves in almost on a daily basis.

All that being said: Enjoy!

As the Duke of Wellington once said: "I don't know what effect these men will have upon the enemy, but by God, they frighten me."

*****

Three Regimental Sergeant Majors from different regiments were having a drink in the mess one day and, as per usual, were boasting about their units. Now each of these men was as hard as flint; done it all; seen it all and brooked no disobedience from their troops.

The Marine R.S.M. says, "I'll show you how hard my lads are." He looks around and spots an unfortunate marine minding his own business. "You!" he cries. "Get a twenty five pound rucksack on your back, run for ten miles and be back here in thirty minutes."

"Sir: Yes sir!" came the reply as the unlucky one snapped to attention. He was off and running, returning in the requisite time.

"See," says the Marine R.S.M: "Hard as nails."

"That's nothin'," replies the R.S.M. from the Parachute Regiment. "You boy: Here!"

A Para trots over in double quick time. You didn't mess with this sergeant. "Sir: Yes sir," he says.

"Get a fifty pound pack on yer back; run twenty miles and get back here in thirty minutes."

The paratrooper is off and running. He makes it – just, coming smartly to attention in front of the three R.S.M.'s.

The Para Sergeant Major is as pleased as punch. "Hard as nails, my lads," he brags confident that his lad's feat couldn't be bettered.

"That's nothin'," boasts the Royal Engineers R.S.M. "Watch this! You! – Sapper! – Here!"

A hapless soldier from the Engineers wanders over in his own good time.

"Get a hundred pound pack on your back. Do two marathons back to back and I'll see you at six in the morning in your number one dress uniform outside the guardroom."

"Sir?" queried the Sapper raising an eyebrow.

"You heard."

"Sir: F*** off; Sir!"

With that the Royal Engineers' man turns to his two colleagues: "Now that's hard as nails!"

THE QUEEN'S SHILLING

I was just sixteen when I took the Queen's Shilling, signing on the dotted line at the Army Recruiting Office in Shrewsbury. And I remember the day well: I was as sick as a parrot.....

There were two of us for interview that morning, the ordeal to be closely followed by something much worse – the written test. I was never very interested in school, so the test paper was daunting. Still, I wanted to be a paratrooper; it's not as if I was trying out for brain surgery in the Medical Corps.

But I was nervous, not over-confident and my dad was waiting downstairs, so I was determined not to fail. Good intentions, but the question paper left me cold. I had no idea what the questions meant let alone know the answers. How to get around the problem? Answer: Copy the guy's answers and, failing that, guess. No harm in that – all I needed was enough marks to get into the Para's, whereas the other lad had been telling me he was after a trade, blah-de-blah.

Time for the result: I was mortified. The recruitment sergeant spoke to him first: "Sorry son. I can only offer you the infantry."

The lad was in tears whereas I'm thinking 'Oh no: If he's only got the infantry, then I've failed for sure.'

"I wanna be a painter and decorator," he was sobbing as the sergeant turned to me. "Well, I can offer you a trade."

My mind is in a whirl. The idiot must have mixed the examination papers up. "I don't want a trade. I wanna be a Para."

"Well, son: You can't. It's the Junior Leaders' Regiment of the Royal Engineers for you."

"But....."

"No 'buts.' You'll see more action as a combat engineer than you ever will jumping out of perfectly good aeroplanes; in any case the Engineers have their own Para's. And they'll give you a trade."

I'll trade all right, I'm thinking. Maybe I can trade jobs with the sobbing creature beside me.

Only that didn't happen.

BASIC BOOTS

The sergeant is bellowing at us new recruits: "I am NOT your friend! Do you understand? You are not to knock on my door every two minutes unless there is a problem - and if there is a problem I only want to hear that you've fixed it. Do you understand?"

We answered as one: "Yes sergeant." All except for one, he was half a second too slow. The word 'sarge' resounded in the silence.

"Sarge! Sarge! I'm a serg-ant. That's my rank. There's only two types of 'sarg' in this mans army; a mass-arge and a saus-arge. Get it right or I'll shove my stick up your pass-arge and run you round the parade ground like a lollipop. And when I say jump I expect to see you up and down like a toilet seat. Understand?"

Excellent news; I can't wait for our first inspection............

*

It's time for a boot inspection during our initial training. We've been at our boots for days and they are in mint condition: Immaculate: We've been lucky; Jacky Simpson from Glasgow is the son of an ex-guardsman and knows all the tricks.

With as much confidence as a bunch of sprogs can muster, we stand by our beds, boots perfectly positioned and presented.

It doesn't take much to smash our assuredness: The sergeant walks in: First bed: "Rubbish," he says to the crestfallen recruit. Next bed: "Rubbish!" Next: "You've got to be having a joke."

Then it's Jacky's turn: "Simpson: Open that window behind you."

Jacky knows what's coming. He's been born and bred Army and has that instinct. He comes to attention; about turns; opens the window – and throws his boots out.

"What did you do that for," asks the sergeant?

"Boots no good, sergeant: Had to throw them out, sergeant."

"The boots were brilliant, you idiot."

Jacky looked quizzical.

"I asked you to open the window because it's hot in here: Pillock!"

Jacky closed his eyes; totally gutted. Two days work lying in ruins two storeys below.

HALLOWED TURF

Now grass is a pretty ordinary thing – something most people have in their garden and something just taken for granted.

Not so, the soldier: Not if you have a Stickman who likes everything just so; and if the queen is coming on a visit, he hits the stratosphere three weeks in advance and doesn't come down. He makes sure everything is painted and cleaned; and ensures everyone is rehearsed to within an inch of screaming point: Then he notices the brown patches on the playing fields; muddy patches thanks to goalmouth scrambles and five metre scrums: And brown will offend the royal eye.

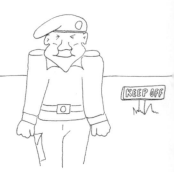

The answer is easy: "Paint the playing fields green:" Then: "Keep off. - Or else!" No one is allowed on the hallowed turf: Soccer is cancelled; rugby is banned – but the SSM is still on edge, continually on the look-out for transgressors.

Twenty four hours to go. This time tomorrow the queen will be here taking tea – and the Stickman is congratulating himself. Everything is in order; he'll get to salute her: He's just about wetting himself with excitement as he stands in the window of his office sipping the final cuppa of the day, when a young squaddie shoots across his line of sight. And he's on the grass.

It was grub time and the young un' was late. A short cut to the cookhouse had seemed a chance worth taking in the gathering gloom.

"That man there! Stand still!" The orders bellowed across the camp.

"Bugger!" murmured the soldier to himself coming to attention. There was no mistaking that voice.

Within seconds the Stickman is 'whispering' in his ear. "You **** idiot:" he's screaming from the road outside his office. "Can't you bleeding read? Get off my bleeding grass: NOW!"

The thunder-struck squaddie starts to run – only to be brought to an abrupt halt: "Don't you bleedin' walk on my bleedin' grass. For every step you take you'll get an extra duty."

Without a pause for reply, the soldier falls to the floor – and rolls the full fifty yards to the road which wound its way through the camp. Once he fell off the kerb edge, the squaddie rose from the gutter - and smartly marches off without a word.

It is rumoured that the Stickman even smiled.

"THE RUSSIANS ARE COMING: THE RUSSIANS ARE COMING!"

2 a.m. The phones are ringing up and down the street. For the hard of hearing, [or the dead drunk,] the regimental guard were racing up front garden paths or clattering up the stairs of countless blocks of flats, their feet resounding in the darkness. Doors are banged and banged again. Kids are crying; bedside lights are coming on all over West Germany.

And the message is the same: "The Russians are coming."

We'd been expecting 'Active Edge' for weeks; trained for it in fact. A full scale exercise to test the readiness of the British Army should the unthinkable happen. Within minutes, squaddies were pouring into the barracks. Bleary-eyed, maybe – but every man knew his job, honed to perfection for just this moment.

It came as no surprise that our unit responded in time-honoured fashion. Not only were the armoured vehicles warming up, churning out an oily filth into the clean night sky, but the communications geeks had done their tweaking and twiddling: Even the kettle was on.

3.30 a.m. The third brew was already under way when the Squadron Sergeant Major marched in. He might be a small guy, but he was nasty with it. And as usual he was starched to within an inch of his life – but tonight we were in for praise. We smile at him, even pointed to the tea pot, but he never moved from the doorway. He was bristling, beyond the red-in-the-face anger we were used to: More white and trembling. Even his swagger stick tucked under his right arm bobbed uncontrollably.

Silence fell: Bacon and egg sandwiches paused half way to gaping mouths; the whistling kettle served only to heighten the silence which had fallen across the assembled crowd.

"You….." he barked. Then continued, using a lot of words ending with 'ing.' None were complementary.

We looked at one another nonplussed. We'd done well: Hadn't we? Vehicles: Communications: We were ready to face down the Russian threat. What else could we do?

"You….." he blasted. "How are you going to kill the Commie sons of bitches without your weapons? Get to the armoury: Now!"

Within minutes we were drawing our rifles: No mean feat as it was five miles away on the other side of Hameln town. And I would swear we could still hear him.

I don't know about the Russians – but if they knew about our Sergeant Major, they'd stay in Moscow.

A RABBIT OUT OF THE HAT

It's mid-winter and we're freezing. Worse: For two days we've been chilled to the bone and starving with hunger since someone in a nice warm office somewhere decided we needed some survival training. And we still had five days to go.

Fortunately, the British Army takes the health and safety of its men seriously; [you can laugh now;] and so we'd endured the classroom bit: How to build a basher for shelter: How to snare game.

It had seemed easy enough – watching an expert in the dry and warm – but our muddy ditch on a wind swept, and frequently snow-dusted moor, was turning nightmarish.

Day One: Was it just yesterday? Dropped off God knows where; fugitives behind enemy lines with a bunch of hard cases from the Para's giving us a six hour head start. But no worries: Our little band of four had found this nice ditch surrounded by a wooded coppice where the heath adjoined some pasture land.

Rule One: Get shelter from the elements – and we reckoned we had a couple of hours before dark: Time enough to set the traps for grub and get the basher up. But things started to go wrong immediately when it came to securing the camouflaged tarpaulin over our hide out. The trees were just too far apart for the elasticated bungee-rope-type securing things to stretch.

Undeterred, we deploy Alf – a bit slow on the uptake, but as strong as an ox. He attaches a second bungee to the first by means of a metal clip; then a third.

"Pull Alfie; pull!" we encourage as his bull shoulders took the strain. Off he went, his iron legs making the distance. It was working. Around the tree he went, the elastic ties becoming tighter and tighter; harder and harder to reach the final securing belay point.

Two feet to go:

One foot:

Then it happened. With a reverberating twang-g-g the bungee elasticated thing snapped, unravelled around the tree and, travelling at the speed of light, first one, then a second metal securing point, hit Alfie smack between the eyes.

He was out for the count. Even before we got to him, a massive cone-like lump was already towering from his forehead. We tried to wake him, but no: Unconsciousness had set in.

'Ah well,' we reasoned: 'Might as well do something useful,' so off we went in search of food.

Nothing doing: We reset the traps and hoped for some luck by morning: Into the ditch dragging poor Alfie in behind us, laying the tarp loosely above our heads.

Alfie was awake by sun-up. And that was okay – we'd been too cold to sleep. More importantly we were thankful he was back with us as no one wanted to go looking for the Para's who'd threatened to do all sorts of unpleasantness to us when they'd flushed us out.

The trouble was, by now, we were hungry enough to eat one another. Moving as best we could to remain unseen, we check the traps. Nothing! Zero! Ziltch: Near to tears, we hold a council of war, squatting in a circle in a small clearing in the wood: 'What to do:' 'What to do:' That sort of thing, when a miracle happened.

A white rabbit: A very large white rabbit hopped into our lives. It didn't seem to have noticed us, quite happy to sit and nibble at the grass.

We all moved – slowly at first, picking up whatever was to hand; basically lumps of half rotted branches and some hand sized stones. "Here bunny, bunny....." What followed wasn't pretty – just necessary.

In short order the rabbit was no more; cooked and devoured with relish, washed down with copious amounts of self satisfaction. We'd remembered our lessons well – especially the part about wasting nothing. So, the rabbit skin, head lolling backwards and tongue hanging loosely, was stretched out to dry; nailed to a tree trunk at the back of the camp.

We were just settling in when one of the Directing Staff sauntered up. He checked we were okay before getting to the real reason for his visit: "If you see a white rabbit it's off limits," he orders. "Do not kill it! Do I make myself clear?"

"Yes, sergeant," we reply in unison.

"It's a pet rabbit which has wandered off from the owner's garden and their kid is real upset."

Something must have shown in Alfie's face.

"What?" challenged the sergeant: "You haven't seen it have you?"

The bang on the head must have done Alfie some good. "No sergeant," he lied; his eyes fixed on the spread-eagled corpse nailed just above the instructor's head.

All thoughts of a nice, warm Davy Crocket fur hat had just disappeared as quickly as its late owner.

It was an ordinary day. Two Sappers and their corporal are on duty at the gates to their camp in Germany: Just three ordinary blokes bored out of their trolleys on a sunny Sunday waiting for their shift to end.

In the distance they can hear the wail of sirens; the local emergency services are doing their stuff, but they are too far away for the army lads to see anything and anyway, it's nothing to do with them.

An hour goes by, then the sirens start up again – and they get closer and closer and closer until a police car comes into view. It's travelling fast heading directly for the squaddies; blue lights, sirens, smoke coming from the brakes: The car tyres squeal as it slides broadside and comes to an abrupt halt.

A single German cop jumps out of his green and white and runs to the unmoving Sappers by the white pole which blocks the entrance to the camp. "Open zee gate! Open zee gate!" He's whizzing, this cop: Really excited.

"Corp," one of the guards shouts, needing advice from someone higher up the chain.

"Open zee gate: Now!" orders the policeman.

"Now then, officer," asks the corporal arriving at the barrier. "What's this all about?"

"You open the gates: Now!"

"Why?"

"You open: Now: Now!" The German cop is literally jumping up and down on the spot in his agitation.

"Sorry: No can do unless you tell….."

The corporal didn't get a chance to finish the sentence. The policeman runs back to his car, opens the door and – no; he doesn't drive away: - He emerges with a revolver in his fist. Pointing it at the three squaddies he says, "You open: Now!"

It wasn't quite the reaction he'd hoped for. Within a split second, three machine guns were levelled at him; the click of the safety catches coming off sounded very loud in the silence.

The policeman was a quick learner. He threw his gun back in the car, raising his hands in surrender whilst shouting, "Don't shoot: Don't shoot!"

N.B: It turned out all that the German cop wanted was to look at the river behind the camp to see if there was a suitable place from which to tackle an oil spill which was coming down stream.

When you are charged with driving an eighty-eight ton Scammell Crusader loaded with two Atlas diggers, you have to take your job seriously.

My mate, Scouse, and I were new to the depot in Northern Ireland, so we made doubly sure everything was hunky-dorey. Firstly the maps: We pour over them. Any bridge lower than sixteen feet in height has to be marked and as our loaded trucks are pretty close to that height, the route has to be planned, then double checked.

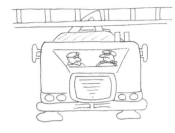

Secondly, there's the load. The two diggers are manoeuvred onto the flat bed of the Scammell, their long arms positioned and tied down: Out comes the tape measure: Fifteen feet ten inches: A two inch breathing space.

We're off. A quarter of a mile from the camp and there's the first bridge; a new pedestrian concrete thing dazzling white in the sun. But we're okay; there's no sign which means it's over sixteen feet.

C-R-A-S-H: The scream of metal travelling at twenty miles an hour as it gouges huge lumps out of the bridge is ear shattering. The Crusader, its diggers and the bridge become intertwined.

There's an enquiry of course: Well, several: Police, Army and Council, but we're exonerated. Our load was correct – the bridge was only fifteen feet six inches high AND there was no sign. The council is in the mire. Not only does it have to pay for all the damage and repairs, but it has to send a team out to put things to rights.

For weeks they scrape the road surface, fiddle with the bridge, until eventually it's ready. It's even had another nice new coat of dazzling white paint.

The day the bridge re-opens, we have an identical job to the one when the accident had happened. The two diggers are loaded, tied down and measured: Fifteen feet ten inches – and we're off.

The bridge is coming up. It looks good; still no road signs, but no matter, they've sorted the problem…..

C-R-A-S-H: The sound of metal on bridge is horrendous accompanied by that sinking feeling in your stomach.

"You've got to be joking," we cry as one.

But it was no joke. We're stuck fast: Again.

Another inquiry and once more we're cleared. The council had effectively heightened the bridge by lowering the road, scraping the tarmac back to the base level. But did they have to put so much tarmac back down…..?

MAD DOG AND ENGLISHMEN

When I was first promoted to full screw, I arrived in a section which had more than its fair share of Scots in its ranks. And these blokes, apart from being hard; speaking a language of their own and being, shall we say, nationalist to the core; had decided they weren't too happy at having an English bloke – me – coming in to take charge.

Fortunately, my parents had compiled our family history tracing me back to the Scottish, Ettrick and Yarrow valleys, the homes of the Hogg, Laidlaw and Scott families. And that's where these hard cases were from: We even drank in the same pub by the loch. So I had no trouble – but…..

That 'but' was Mad Dog who had a sense of humour to test a Saint. We're on exercise – training for the real thing: Full body kit; respirator on and carrying eighty pounds on our backs. The rucksacks were so heavy that you had to lie down to put them on; then get two of your mates to pull you to your feet.

We'd trudged five miles in the burning heat on our way to the next 'task area,' Mad Dog taking point. All of a sudden, at the top of a rise, he kneels down; arm gesturing to 'Get down!'

We hit the deck, personal weapons at the ready. It probably looked good; real professional to any observer: Only Mad Dog didn't move.

The sergeant wiggles his way forward in a belly crawl. "What's up, Jock?" he asks in a broad Geordie accent.

"Nothin'," Mad Dog answers as he stands up. "Just wanted to see a bunch of English ****'s get on their knees for a Jock."

He wanders off, leaving thirty of us stranded like upside down turtles, unable to get back to our feet.

A SCABBY CHRISTMAS

It was fast approaching Christmas and I was one of the unlucky ones. Someone had to make sure things ticked over in camp and so two of us Engineers were volunteered: Me and a Geordie bloke from Newcastle.

Christmas looked far from being a cheery affair, but at least with so few of us around, things were pretty relaxed. Billy and I took turns to pop out of camp for fags and other essentials and on Christmas Eve, it was my turn.

"Are you at the camp?" asked this attractive, twenty-some year old as I queued by the till in the newsagents. She wasn't fey: I was in full uniform.

"Yeah: All over Christmas."

"Are you on your own?"

"No, my mate Billy is stuck over the holidays to."

"Tell you what," she said. "Come to my house for Christmas dinner. Both of you: Twelve o'clock," she added as she scribbled her address down.

"Thanks very much," I said. "We'll not be missed for a couple of hours."

Next day: Billy and I showered; put on our best uniforms and headed for the house of the kind lady. We were invited in, asked to go into the homely and warm, front room-cum-dining room, and handed a beer.

Great: We were enjoying ourselves chatting with her as she popped in and out setting the lunch table. In due course the meat arrived; a huge plate of pork with loads of crunchy, salty skin, all surrounded by roast tatties and veg.

"Be back in a minute," the kind lady said, so we decided to drain our beers in readiness for the feast, and that's when her ten year old lad came in. It was the first time we'd seen him and it did come as a bit of a nasty surprise: He was shaven headed; his face and scalp being covered in sores; some with brown scabs formed over them and some still suppurating. He leaned over the plate and started picking at the meat, moving the veggies out of the way with a finger that, moments before, had been picking at the scabs.

He grabbed a nice looking piece of pork and was gone.

Billy looked at me and said what we both were thinking: "I don't fancy any of that, mate. Not with Scab boy having had his fingers all over it."

I agreed. It was a real turn-off, but I didn't have any idea what to do about it.

But Billy did. Being a Geordie he was, shall we say, forthright: Not that there's anything wrong with that; my parents are Geordies, but when the nice lady entered the room, he came right out with it: "I'm sorry missus, but where ah cum frae, wi al-wiz ha' wor puddin' forst. It's tradition ye na'."

I translated his lie: Geordies have their Christmas pudding first. It's tradition. And to give the lady her due, she agreed to serve the pudding first to make her guests feel at home.

It was a big, traditional pudding, complete with a huge jug of custard. We got stuck into it and did it justice. Then we had seconds; might as well fill up on something as the pork dinner didn't take our fancy any more.

We sat back, full as guns.

"Right, lads: I'll bring your dinners in," said the astonished, nice lady.

"Well," says Geordie. "Hang on a second, there. I can't say I was best pleased when your son came in and raided the meat plate. Put us off a bit."

"I'm really sorry: Harold," she shouts! "Get yourself in here."

Scabby Harold turns up looking a bit sheepish, still picking at the irritating skin disease.

"Did you come in here and help yourself to the pork?"

"Yes Mam."

"Well you're very naughty. And while I'm at it, where's your headscarf the doctor said you had to wear to keep those sores covered?"

"My headscarf," he queried?

"Yes: Where is it? Put it on."

"I can't Mam. You cooked the Christmas pudding in it."

THE SPANISH INQUISITION

Bavaria: It's deep mid-winter and just the sort of weather the guys behind desks love to organize Escape and Evasion courses: Snow: Wind: And bitterly cold.

On this particular course, [Long Range Recognisance] organized by the British S.A.S., were special forces from Germany, Holland, America; all over the place in fact – including our own blokes.

Our job was to make up the 'Hunter Force,' and once we'd been kitted up with Land Rovers, thermal-imaging equipment and night vision binoculars, off we went to capture these men of the Special Forces – who incidentally, had absolutely no intention of being caught. Basically, they'd do anything during their sixty kilometre hike to avoid us: They knew what to expect from the professional interrogators waiting for them back at camp.

It's dusk; snow is in the air, and we're bouncing along a muddy and pot-holed track just five k's short of the zone boundary when, out of the corner of my eye, I see a movement; no more than the briefest of shadows in the tree line.

"Bobby!" I shout in the Sergeant's ear. "Tree line: Four o'clock."

I was really pleased with myself for spotting the guy 'on the run,' as it had only been hours earlier that I'd cocked our O.P. up. We'd done a real good job on that O.P. as well – Land Rover cam'd up; tyres and footprints obliterated: It was as near perfect a set up as you could get – until I had to rescue some binoculars from the vehicle. As I reached through the driver's door and stretched…..I hit the horn. It shattered the silence – and just because some idiot had forgotten to switch off the electrics under the dash. And that idiot was me.

So, I was determined to make amends as the Land Rover skidded to a halt; then reversed at speed toward the trees.

We pile out. "Look for his tracks," I shout – hardly rocket science seeing as how the snow was lying in drifts up here on the fence line surrounding the plantation. Seconds later we're diving into the trees following two sets of tracks. Two sets of tracks was good news as these exercises always had the 'escapees' travelling in pairs.

After fifty yards, the tracks separate. And now it is pitch black, thanks to the towering and thickly planted trees. There are three of us in our patrol – and seeing as how I had something to prove, off I went on my own.

The tracks ended at the base of a massive tree: He's either behind it – or up it. And that puts me in a pickle: These are Special Forces guys we're hunting – and one on one wouldn't be a fair fight – on me that is, so I start screaming, "I got him. I got him."

My mates are crashing through the trees toward me – but our quarry is off and running like a stag.

Unfortunately for him, I was into rugby in a big way at the time, and felled him with a text book tackle. He was doubly unlucky: He landed on his head in the snow, only the snow was covering a log. He gave it a right crack; blood spurting every which way. I was onto him, but even semi-conscious, he was fighting like a man possessed. But my two mates were there within seconds – and that was that. The plasti-cuffs on his wrists were so tight they drew blood, but despite it all, he struggled to stop us getting him into the back of the Land Rover; then struggled to try and throw himself out. All he got for his efforts was a couple of kicks in the ribs.

"Where's your mate?"

"Keh-keh?" He didn't understand.

"Where – eest – yer – friend?"

"Keh-keh," he replied looking stupid?

"Frend – o. Where is….." Oh **** it: Kick-kick.

He's near to breaking point; freezing cold, bleeding, but we can't get a thing out of him except, "Keh-keh." He spots a half-eaten doughnut on the dashboard: He's nodding toward it giving it plenty of 'Keh-keh's'. He sounded just like Manuel out of Fawlty Towers.

"Sorry: No food-o," and with that a sandbag was stuck over his head.

We arrive back at camp and chuck him out the back door, where he lands at the feet of the S.A.S. Sergeant: "Well done, lads," he congratulates us as he pulls our prisoner upright by his hair roots. "Now: Let's see what you've got here." The sandbag is pulled off. "What is THAT!" the S.A.S. guy asks, looking over in our direction?

We just look stupid: What's he talking about? "He's one of yours ain't he?" we ask a little uncertainly now, all looking at our sergeant, Bobby - he had more stripes than us.

"I've never seen this bloke before in my life. He's not one of mine. Take IT back where you found IT," he ordered.

"But he's bleeding like a stuck pig….."

"Then stick a bandage on and get rid," he replied, walking off. "If I see him again, you three can go meet MY interrogators.

One huge bandage, several doughnuts and heaps of coffee later we're back at the tree line with 'Keh-Keh.'

"Out you get, mate."

"Keh?"

"You – go – now - o." All said very slowly so he'll understand.

"Keh?"

"Out – Out!"

 Now he understands. "Na-na-na." You can tell he's on our wave length now – his white knuckles and fingers buried deep into the back of the seat is a dead give-away. He's no intention of getting out: He's staying put. He's warm – and fed – and he's had enough.

I felt sorry for him – for the fear in his eyes – for a whole second, until the S.A.S. Sergeant's words flooded back. "If I see him again….."

Three of us drag him out the back. He's screaming and kicking and fighting: Then he's in the bottom of a ditch. We're jumping into the back of an already moving Land Rover. He's running after us shouting, "Na-na-na."

We reckon he must be asking for another doughnut – and oblige by throwing a bagful at him as we disappear into the snowy night.

PS: We found out later our 'prisoner' was a Spanish Air Force officer on a different exercise. Whoops!

Our guide was to be the Canadian padre. He was the only one to know his way around this part of the Rocky Mountains and assured us he could find us grizzly bears.

Now, the padre was a good bloke, his twenty-stone frame being home to a brilliant sense of humour. We'd been told that he'd once been in the Canadian navy and when the new destroyer Captain took his command out of the harbour for the first time our padre had unfurled a massive 'L' plate from the stern – right in front of the watching Admiral.

He found the grizzlies for us, and then warned of just how dangerous an animal they could be. Of course that was a challenge to the ten of us young soldiers. We were out of the mini bus in a flash, getting close enough to their smelly coats and worse smelling teeth; close enough so that their bulk filled the camera lenses.

Back on the bus the padre deals with our rashness by way of a story: Two men are out on a hunting trip when they come across a grizzly. One man sits down on a rock and proceeds to take off his boots replacing them with a pair of trainers he's had dangling around his neck. "It's no good," says his friend. "You'll never outrun a grizzly." "I've no intention of outrunning the bear," he replies: "Just so long as I can outrun you."

Twenty years later, I reckon we were lucky playing chicken with those creatures, but the padre's story and warnings must have had some effect even then.

We'd set up camp that night in a clearing provided by the National Parks Department and not so very far from the mini bus. The padre takes a trenching spade and saunters off 'to the heads' as the navy men would say.

He's gone for a while – long enough for one or two of us to start wondering what he's doing in the darkness.....

Just at that point of decision as to whether to start hunting for him or not, this huge figure of a man runs through the camp, toilet roll in one hand, spade in the other, shouting, "Holy Shit!"

We took the hint and ran like Olympic athletes to the bus. Only we'd overtaken the padre and the vehicle doors were locked. In ill-disguised panic, we pull at the handles.

It took ages to realise the padre hadn't turned up, so we carefully retrace our steps only to find him having a beer by the fire.

"So you believed me about the running shoes then?" he asked as he smiled, burped and tossed the empty tin on the pile.

For three days we hadn't slept other than for a 'power wob' as the instructors called it. Ten minutes here and there to keep you going. Only there comes a time when trees begin to walk around talking to one another, or, in the case of one squaddy, a tube train roared down on him from out of the forest. So real was it, that the soldier could describe the driver in great detail: And he did as we hoisted him out of the twenty feet deep crevice he'd thrown himself into to get out of the train's way.

It was the Pennines; the rough bits on the fell tops in January, but not even the cold, or the threat of other units having been ordered to attack us, could stave off sleep. We were even sleeping standing up, and I have to admit I'd dozed off.

I had no idea where I was, only someone was shaking my shoulder and saying in my ear, "Your turn for stag, Pat. Over there."

By the time I was semi-conscious, he'd gone and I'd no idea where my sentry duty, 'over there' was. 'I'll go this way,' I said to myself and staggered off whispering, "Hello: Hello: Anyone there," into the darkness.

I was fully awake when the first trip flare went off. "Shit!" I swore to myself bending down to untangle the wire from my boot.

Flares were going up. The sentries opened fire with their s.m.g's: Thunder-flashes went off: Soldiers were running about this way and that; everyone shouting: "Where are they?" "Over there!" "Over here!"

And I'm thinking, 'I'm in the kak now,' when a sentry ran passed. "You see 'em Pat?"

"Yeah: They went that way," I lied and joined in the search for the 'enemy' units who'd tried and failed to break the security around our positions.

The Commanding Officer was really pleased we'd repelled the attack, but must have scratched his head when unit after unit of the 'enemy' troops reported in: "It wasn't us: We couldn't even find them."

A SIGHT FOR SORE EYES

The Directing Staff were not pleased. You can always tell these things - and as fifty of us were lined up in the desert as naked as the day we were born.....

It was a survival exercise: More rabbits and pigeons awaited, but we'd thought to liven our rations up a bit. Only we got caught. A shame really as we'd taken hours to iron dozens of Mars Bars to the consistency of pancakes before sewing them into our uniforms. Only the blistering sun had melted the chocolate; the resultant stains giving the game away.

So there we were being given a right shelaking about fairness and decency, when a hot air balloon appears out of nowhere, passing over us at no more than fifty feet off the ground. The basket is crammed full of holiday makers – a school trip by the looks of it: a girl's school – and the fourteen and fifteen year olds were making a right old noise.

"Get yer kit on," came the order, but what the observers thought of fifty naked men running about or hopping on one leg as they tried to get their trousers back on, heaven only knows.

Only Mad Dog has to be different. He jumps onto a pile of rocks and shouts: "Last chicken in Sainsbury's."

Escape and Evasion techniques: The A – Z of body-guarding: High Speed driving:

Did I say 'high speeds?' Moron! For 'high' read suicidal – especially if my mate 'Champ,' [as in Champion the Wonder Horse; but that's another story,] was at the wheel.

On these 'high speed days' we'd go out, four up, in our vehicle: Three students taking it in turns to drive whilst the instructor got greyer and greyer by the hour.

It was Champ's turn to drive and we're belting along a public road across Salisbury Plain. It's undulating with plenty of dips – but straight. And Champ was giving a running commentary as directed, just like the cops do on their advanced courses.

"Mirror: Signal: Checking mirror: Overtaking now: My speed is 125 mph: I will remain in the offside lane to overtake the line of slow-moving lorries crawling up the next hill."

The instructor twitched. There was a lorry – only this one had just appeared from one of those dips in the road I told you about, and was heading straight for us.

Champ was not concerned: "A vehicle has appeared in front of us some 200 yards away: At this speed I should be able to make the gap between the next two lorries on the nearside of the carriageway."

I was still thinking about the use of the word 'should', when: "Brake Champ!" The instructor put a restraining hand on his forearm and again said matter-of-factly, "Brake Champ."

"We can make it," the driver said, keeping his foot on the accelerator.

"Brake!"

"We can make it," Champ replies and keeps going.

"Brake: Brake: For *'s sake; Brake!" The instructor is screaming as the approaching wagon fills our windscreen.

Champ's voice never altered from the monotone. "We're braking now to reduce speed at the point of impact."

The front of our high-powered car dipped violently, clouds of smoke billowing from the front tyres: A jerk of the steering wheel and we're back on our correct side of the road – only we're two feet from the rear of the lorry in front and two feet from the front of the one behind.

"Overtake now complete," drones Champ. "Moving out: Looking to overtake….."

Mad Dog was…..an individual; that's the polite way of putting it: A Scottish Nationalist through and through who didn't like taking orders, so he'd continually mutter, "Yer bastard," under his breath at anyone who was telling him what to do. And, for Mad Dog, work was something to be avoided at all costs; not a trait which endeared him universally, especially should you be paired off with him in a task involving physical labour.

It was my turn to have him.

"Dig in on the top of that hill," the lieutenant ordered.

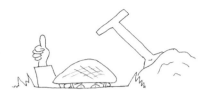

"Yer bastard," muttered Jock.

"It must be six feet deep," the officer continues.

"Yer bastard."

"…..live in it for two days."

"Yer bastard."

We were the last two blokes in a long line of trenches being dug in front of our defensive positions. Whilst I set to, digging like a rabbit, Mad Dog lies down next to the growing hole in the ground and stares into space.

After three feet, I'm done for. The exhaustion got a whole lot worse when I realized that I'd just hit solid rock. There was no way I'd get much further without using explosives – and that was as likely as Mad Dog Jock using his shovel.

The sergeant comes over to see how 'we' are getting on.

"Impossible, sergeant," I said, hitting the rock with my spade.

"Shut your face and dig," he ordered, as he turned about and left. I reckon he'd had a bad day.

"Yer bastard," says Jock, as the figure disappears.

I begin digging again.

"You're wasting your firkin time," says Mad Dog in his best Scottish accent.

I manage another six inches by scraping away all the loose shale before I spot the lieutenant and sergeant heading our way. They were stopping and checking each trench in turn.

"Oh no," I groaned. "We're in the shit, Jock."

We were both standing behind the trench when the nice, smart young officer strides across, his sergeant now hurrying to keep up. "Well lads….."

"Finished sir," says Mad Dog.

"Let me see then," the officer replies, but before he can move forward to inspect the miserable hole in the ground, Jock jumps into the trench landing on his knees and sinks down on his haunches as far as is possible. Only his eyes are above the lip of our hole.

"Well done, young man," says the officer: "Best of the lot."

"Thank you, sir," I reply.

"Yer bastard," mumbles Jock at the departing figures. The aloud: "Told you not to worry, Pat."

CHILDS EYE VIEW

Northern Ireland: A patrol of Royal Marines are resting, backs against a wall of an R.U.C. station in Fermanagh, when a seven year old sidles up bouncing a football. He stands silently in front of one of the marines whose turn it was to strip down his rifle; and watches as he carefully cleans it before putting the sight to his eye.

"That's a SUSAT sight," the seven year old says knowledgably.

"You know your stuff," replied the marine amicably.

Another bounce or two of the ball: "I'll bet you I can strip your SA 80 down quicker than you," the little footballer challenges.

"Phhh!" exclaimed the whole patrol with a dismissive laugh.

"Can to," said the little lad taking exception to the laughter coming in his direction.

"Go on then, son," said the Corporal in charge. "He's bloody useless," indicating the marine who'd been cleaning his weapon. "You'll have no trouble." Making sure the weapon was safe, the Corporal hands the SA 80 over. "I'll time you: Three-two-one: Go!"

Twenty four seconds: [including the breech block.]

The marines are staggered. This kid's an expert. How on earth…..

"Oh! My uncle's got one just like this. He keeps it behind the wardrobe in his bedroom."

"And where does he live..?"

"Just there….."

The marines follow the little pointed finger at the mid-terrace house opposite…..

"Have a piece of chocolate, son….."

FEATHERS AT GOOSE LAKE

It used to be a Hitler youth camp and unfortunately it was still being run in much the same fashion by a General in the Belgium Army. It's fair to say he wasn't liked.

We'd been sent to this training area on the Belgian border with Germany for a bit of gunnery practice and were happy to find we were mixing with soldiers from Germany, Belgium and Holland – a good bunch who enjoyed a drink and a laugh after work. [Between bed inspections and parades of varying descriptions dreamed up by the Commandant.]

The gunnery range itself was set high on a cliff, the weaponry being discharged across a huge lake. The location was ideal; we could fire away until our hearts were content. Okay so far? But…..and there's always a 'but:' our 'but' was the general. He was crazy about birds. Not only did he have his own loft of very valuable racing and breeding pigeons; his pride and joy, but any sign of wildlife on the lake below the gun emplacements, and we had to stop shooting. Injure so much as a sparrow and you'd be lucky to escape the hangman's noose.

So there we were, firing off our bipod mounted heavy calibre machine guns, when three Canada geese dropped in making perfect landings in the middle of the lake. Under normal circumstances we'd have taken a smoko – but being pulled out of bed early, [again,] for yet another inspection – well…..

And our corporal and S.S.M. were having a brew…..And the geese, now feeding with their backsides in the air, were very tempting. The devil got his way and three machine guns opened up. The tracers arched over the water.

But the birds were not stupid. They were up on their tip toes, running across the water, wings flapping, trying to take off.

You could see the bullets hitting the water: The faster the birds ran, the faster the bullets caught them up.

The first bird is up; then the second. I swear they were zigzagging like World War 2 bombers avoiding flak. Alas Tail-End Charlie, number three, didn't make it; the bird exploding in a cloud of feathers.

The culprits glance over toward the supervisors who were still blissfully unaware of the carnage below, and I reckon we'd have got away with it if it hadn't been for some lads in the German Army.

They were bored and harbouring a grudge against the bird-fancying general, so decided to break into his pigeon coop. I suppose things got a little out of hand in there as some half-wit decided that the birds would do better without their heads: This one mongrel bit the heads off three pigeons before his mates dragged him out.

We know all this because the story came out that evening over a few beers. The more beer – the funnier it got.

The repercussions came quickly. At first light our Sergeant Major turfed us out of the nice warm barracks to form up in our underpants on the parade ground. One of our mob, Tony, guessed what was coming – an interrogation about murdered pigeons – so he makes a hole in his pillow and stuffs a handful of feathers into his mouth.

The sergeant is going crazy; red faced and bristling. We're in three lines with Tony in the centre of the rearmost one. The sergeant stops in front of every man: starting front line; farthest left as per usual. He puts his nose two inches away from each squaddy's face and stares into his eyes as he asks the question: "Did you bite the heads off those bleedin' pigeons?"

Each man answers truthfully: "Sir: no, Sir; no."

Tony's turn: "Sir: no, sir; no." Only his answer was accompanied by a flurry of feathers.

The parade crumpled in laughter.

"My office: Now."

Tony marched off, still with a trail of feathers behind him as he tried to clear his mouth. Even the S.S.M. managed a smile: "Nice one, lads."

HALF MAN, HALF MAGGOT

A new lad joins the Motor Transport Section – a sprog – and sprogs have a hard time initially; at least until they show they can take a joke.

And it's not long before the squadron is heading out into the boondocks of rural Germany on exercise. The sprogs first taste of life away from the barracks – and little things you take for granted, like electricity and toilets.

First night, and after grub the young soldier feels the need 'to go:' 'A number two.'

"Where do I….." [You get the idea.]

"Take that short spade – and when you've finished, dig a hole and bury it."

A puzzled look:

"Come on, lad: Don't they teach you anything in training: Can't leave any signs or smells for the enemy to find."

"Okay." And off he goes into the bushes.

Within seconds a well planned operation swings into action. A long handled shovel appears and one of the Sappers creeps after the sprog who is settling down to squat, trousers around his ankles. The long handled shovel is eased out – silently – inch by inch, until it is placed beneath the unsuspecting soldier.

Success: The 'jobby' is captured on the shovel; quickly and silently withdrawn.

Satisfied, the sprog stands up, pulling at his clothing, and as he does so, turns to inspect what he'd just parted with. Only it wasn't there: No sign of it; none at all. He peered at the ground. He peered into his clothing, now back around his knees. His puzzlement grew and grew. He shuffles further and further a-field looking in bush after bush, until he's twenty feet away from the scene of the crime.

Still puzzled, he returns to the guys at the overnight camp – who, with commendable straight faces, begin to tell of stories involving a particular German monster: A turd thief who stalks the woods in search of victims.

I think the talk of monsters must have given the new lad nightmares – not that he'd admit to it – because during the night he'd tossed and turned so much that he'd knotted his maggot (sleeping bag) around him. He just couldn't get out and spent a claustrophobic couple of hours whimpering to himself until the dawn arrived.

Well – if you can't take a joke, you shouldn't have joined.

THE NORWAY GREYHOUNDS

Here's a story from yesteryear.

A good friend of my father's served in a northern regiment during the Second World War. They were quickly mobilized and sent as part of the force to face the Germans in Norway. Once there, they marched fifty miles through knee deep snow in single file. As the lead person collapsed exhausted from the trail blazing, the next man in line took over. And they marched fast.

Just as quickly, they were chased out of Norway by the enemy who had complete air superiority. Every move the men made was shadowed by a German sea-plane. So neurotic did one sergeant become, one Charlie Day; that he was awarded the nickname; 'See-Plane Charlie;' 'cos every time he saw an aeroplane, he completely freaked out.

Back in Scotland, the exhausted and defeated regiment were sent to a tented camp outside Hawick where they found themselves in the tender care of a captain who hadn't seen any action at all – but was as near neurotic as Charlie. Only the captain's problem revolved around the threat from German paratroopers landing on the town.

He'd decided that the way to defeat the invaders was to take command of a knob

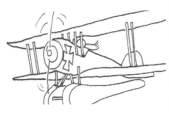

on top of a hill outside the camp. If they came, that's where everyone would head for; but since you couldn't leave the single machine gun out on the hill overnight, [the locals would probably have it away,] it had to be hauled up and back every time.

Half-twelve at night and the captain turns up: "Call out the guard: Call out the guard: Germans are coming: Get the machine gun to the knoll: Come on: Come on: Hurry, hurry, hurry."

So the Norway Greyhounds set to, lugging the machine gun up the steep hill, setting it up; dismantling it; lugging it back to camp: Only they weren't quick enough.

"Do it again:"

"Do it again:"

And again:

And each time the exhausted men were getting slower and slower. By 5 a.m. it was over and the men went to bed. Unfortunately they were due back on parade at six. Fortunately, they had Sergeant See-Plane Charlie who'd been unable to sleep since Norway; the buzzing of the German plane was forever in his head. And he was a compassionate man.

He obeyed his orders. He turned out at 6 a.m. He called the men to attention; inspected the parade and then drilled the men for the ten minutes as prescribed by the captain. "Right turn: Quick march. By the left.....turn:" The whole gambit.

He was still drilling; still barking commands, when the captain left his tent to head for the toilets. For a while the senior officer was pleased to know that the men were being kept at it, but on his way back to his quarters, he thought he was still dreaming. In fact he smacked his own face to make sure he wasn't.

The parade was still going strong: "Left-right-left-right....." But the only person present was See-Plane Charlie; the rest of the men still in bed and snoring their heads off.

THE AXE MAN COMMETH

The old wind-ups have run their course. Even the most retarded sprog straight out of initial training won't fall for: "Go get some tartan paint," or "Ask the store-man for a long weight." So it's necessary to become more and more inventive.

Rodney, a youngster with a baby face and a pencil thin frame which made him duck every time he had to pass through a doorway, arrives for his first day. And like everyone else, he's keen to impress, arriving in front of the lance corporal in polished boots and pressed uniform.

"Okay, Rodney: First job;" began the lance-jack: "I want you to return that axe to the stores for me," he says pointing at the implement in the corner. "It's signed out in my name."

"Right, corporal," Rodney answers pleased to be of some use. He lifts the three feet long axe easily; holding it just where the head meets the shaft.

"It would be better if you carried it over your right shoulder – like we do when drilling with our rifles."

"Yes, corporal:" And off he went, marching smartly.

However, before he gets to the end of the corridor, his N.C.O. appears in the doorway behind him: "Hang on Rodney. You may as well take this envelope with you: It's for the S.S.M. His office is right next to the stores. Only make sure he reads the report before you hand the axe back in, will you?"

"Certainly, corporal:" Sapper Rodney leaves; letter in one hand and the large tree-felling axe smartly in place over his right shoulder.

Five minutes later and he's standing in front of the Squadron Sergeant Major. The senior man keeps the youngster waiting; he doesn't even look up as he's up to the elbows in work; files and reports covering his polished desk with its red leather inlay. And the sergeant is proud of his desk – it had taken him a lifetime in the army to begin to accumulate the trappings of success.

Eventually, he raises one eyebrow and the sapper, coming to attention, axe over his shoulder, hands the envelope across.

The message read:

*"Please give me five extra duties now – or I'm going to chop yer **** desk in half."*

It's not recorded what the busy S.S.M. thought of the matter.

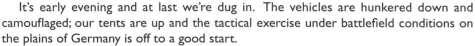

It's early evening and at last we're dug in. The vehicles are hunkered down and camouflaged; our tents are up and the tactical exercise under battlefield conditions on the plains of Germany is off to a good start.

But we're having to rough it: Battlefield conditions means no lights – not even a cigarette is allowed, and to make events as real as possible, we have to hoist our huge Bergens onto our backs and walk eight miles in the darkness to collect our grub: A rabbit and a chicken; both with their clothes still on.

JUST ANOTHER SATURDAY NIGHT WITH THE BOYS

Off we go, desperate for food, a brew and a fag – not necessarily in that order. It was pitch black - then a mirage appeared in the distance. Were we hallucinating? Not a bit of it: It WAS a pub – and sitting there all alone at the side of this little road in the middle of nowhere.

It took one exchange of looks and we were in: Crisps and beer in hand we retreat to the darkened beer garden out the back: Well, we were operating under battlefield conditions.

One delicious icy cold sip before a rustling in the bushes brought our elation crashing to earth: Oh, no: It had to be the cunning so and so of a sergeant out to trap us.

But no: A head popped out: "It's okay lads; it's just Pat and the boys." Relief all around: Pure, unadulterated joy. Get another round in: Plenty of laughter – but we'd learned a lesson: Post a look-out – even if he did have a litre glass in his hand.

Well, we are operating under tactical, battlefield conditions.

Just as well: "C.O.'s coming down the road!"

Within seconds, we're all deep in the bushes. Silence reigns until the senior officer's footsteps have long gone, but he's heading for the food distribution centre.

We're off: Double-quick time, smartly saluting the boss-man as we march passed. The Commanding Officer welcomed our urgency, obviously impressed by the attitude of his men to make this exercise a resounding success. Only we have our own agenda: We have to pass the pub on the way back.

10 p.m. And all of us rabbiteers are back in the beer garden where the locals were impressed with the ingenuity of their allies: Plenty of good humoured banter, laughter and beer.

Time to go: The German licensee phones for the taxis, and after a few minutes we stagger to the waiting vehicles and force our way in. There were so many blokes in the cars that the Bergens, bedecked with dead chickens and rabbits, had to be held outside the vehicle through the open windows.

Our taxi driver thought this was hilarious and agreed to drive the last fifty yards into camp without lights: Well, we're operating under battlefield conditions. He was so taken up by the spirit of adventure that he then decided to deliver each of us to our own appointed hole in the ground, whispering "Goodnight," as we slid away into the darkness.

The last we saw of our Good Samaritan was the vehicle slowly picking its way over rough ground toward the distant road – without lights, of course. Well – he was operating under battlefield conditions.

DIGGER

We're in Cyprus, our troop working on widening a track into an area which was to be used in a forthcoming exercise.

One of our happy-band was a big lad; six feet – eight tall if he was an inch; an affable, good natured giant who could do the work of six men. Give him a shovel and tell him to move a mountain of sand and gravel from A-B and he was your man.

Now my uncle, when he worked at the railway yards, used to have a bloke like Digger: A hard worker, only in his case it was "Wash that train:" But you had to catch him when he got back to the starting point – or he'd keep on going round and around; doing it all again and again.

And Digger was a bit like that. We'd been told of the dangers of working in this part of Cyprus. The local inhabitants were two inch long carnivorous wasps with an orange hoop around their back-ends. They were dangerous – get stung three times and you were medi-vac'd off the island.

So when Digger dug up a nest of these things, he worsened the situation by attacking the first one out of the hole with a pick axe. He swung and missed – just. The wasp disappeared back down into the hole, only to return in thirty seconds with a whole bunch of his mates. They set about Digger who was swinging his axe at them, trying desperately to fend them off.

He wasn't so dull to realise quite quickly he needed help, so began running toward us shouting. Only we couldn't help – we were running for the protection of the distant army transport.

*

But Digger's good nature certainly made you want to look out for him. He was like a ten year old boy trapped in a huge body: You'd have say to him: "Don't touch that or it'll kill you;" but stand back and watch him: He'd wait for a while, then look around to see if anyone was looking, then go to touch it. That was Digger.

So when we got off the boat from Cyprus for a bit of rest and relaxation [R & R] in Egypt, the Land of the Pharaoh's and all that advertising rubbish, I said to him: "Just follow me. Do not under any circumstances start trying to buy anything off the street traders: Right?"

He nods. Fifteen seconds later, I look behind me and there he is engrossed in conversation with an Egyptian child selling Hessian sacks, badly stencilled with pyramids: Everything was a quid. He hands over a ten pound note to the urchin, no doubt expecting to receive some change, but the youngster looks at the big man; then the note; snatches back the bag and takes off. He's worked out that Digger will never catch him.

"He's got me money," Digger shouts, and starts running after him.

We shake our heads in disbelief: Do we follow? We didn't have enough time to make a decision: Running wildly toward us, arms waving every which way, comes the big man – closely pursued by any number of angry Arabs. He's shouting – only we couldn't help – we're running for the safety of the army bus.

*

We get to the pyramids:

"Now: Listen carefully, Digger," I say to him.

"I wanna' camel ride."

"Listen: Listen: That camel driver over there has just demanded five quid off me for taking his animal's picture. Don't go on your own. We'll all do it together. Do you understand?"

"Yes, Pat."

"Good: Now follow me."

I walk twenty yards to the foot of the pyramids to get my photo taken by one of the other guys; turn around – and there's Digger perched on top of a camel.

We go back for him.

"Let me down: Let me down," he's shouting at the bloke holding onto this green saliva dripping animal.

"You give me ten pound or you no get down," the Arab guy is shouting back.

"Let me down!"

"Ten pound:"

It cost a fiver, but we got him back: Lucky, or what! Read on and see:

Back in the centre of Cairo and the President of Egypt was on the move across the city. That meant every street was closed down and the traffic jam increased by the second.

Our lieutenant lets us disembark for a fag: Might as well as we aren't going anywhere for a good while.

Digger wanders away from the bus to see what's going on. What had attracted him was a taxi that had pulled up on the junction and the driver wasn't a happy chappy. For some reason, he sat there with his hand on the horn of the car: As if it was going to help…..

With the big man watching closely, an Egyptian cop wanders over and begins a heated argument with the driver. The taxi man loses it; reverses at speed away from the cop – only he hasn't noticed the old guy with sticks crossing the road behind him. The pedestrian goes down with the car parked on top of him.

Digger's mouth falls open and a frown creases his forehead as two plain clothes security men emerge from the crowd and, together with the uniformed cop, drag the taxi driver out into the roadway and start to kick seven bells out of him.

Digger's brain is working overtime: 'This-is-not-right,' it's saying to him and he's off, heading for the melee. But this time, instead of running away from him, we're after him, grabbing him by the collar and running him backwards into the safety of the bus.

He's a good lad; his heart is in the right place, but I doubt his intervention would have been welcomed: By anyone.

JACK MARRINS' MIND-BLOWING MACHINE

Jacky Marrins was an ordinary bloke. He was average height, average weight; average looks and would never stand out in a crowd. He did his job as a Sapper-driver, and that was that: Until…..

Of course, 'until' - the day he became a legend; just happened to be on the day I was acting as his co-driver whilst delivering a load of rubble to go into the foundations of a new, heli-landing pad at a base outside Newry in Northern Ireland.

We arrive at the gate having chatted amicably on our way to load up and then again on our way to the base. Everything was normal. At the camp gate, we receive directions, and we're off. Only after a few yards, we are faced with a Stickman standing in the middle of the main thoroughfare – and he's pointing with his stick down a side road.

The reason was obvious, [at least to me:] Behind him was several hundred yards of newly laid, still steaming, tarmac – and peering closely at it, were a whole lot of Big Brass complete with their hangers-on.

We don't move. Jacky's face is set in stone – and with eyes staring directly ahead; he begins to rev our lorry's engine.

The Stickman is at his door, tapping on the window with the end of his cane. "That way," he orders.

The engine revs grow in reply.

The window is rapped again.

Jacky locks his door and stares ahead.

I'm looking a bit old-fashioned at Jacky by this time: We're heading for trouble.

The Stickman is going red in the face: He rat-tat-tats; rat-tat-tats, on Jacky's window. He's insistent: He's screaming: I can even hear him above the noise of the screeching of the engine. "Open this **** door: Now!"

I implore Jacky: "Please….."

I breathe a sigh of relief as Jacky winds his window down – but he stops after an inch. "**** ***; you jumped up ****** ******; before I stick that cane up your arse:" Then winds the window back up.

My chest is as tight as a drum. The SSM is really jumping now: First up and down – then sideways as the revs reach a new high. The handbrake is still on; smoke is pouring from our tyres. I don't know what to think; what to do. All I knew was that a whole world of grief was about to descend on us.

But I needn't have worried – Jacky Marrins' had a plan. It may not be a very good plan, but…..

But he released the handbrake – and we shot forward – straight onto the newly re-surfaced road. We were travelling at forty in no time flat, swerving from side to side. The tarmac was in heaps; waves of the stuff headed for the Top Brass: And today they abandoned all pretence of being in control – and ran – but not as fast as the Sergeant Major who was chasing the truck.

At the end of the new road, Jacky stopped our lorry, and with a, "That's fixed that, then;" dropped out of the cab.

The last I heard of Jacky, was that he was flower arranging in a secure unit somewhere.

Another survival exercise: We all reckoned the army enjoys to see its soldiers suffer – but this time it really went over the top.

First: The S.A.S. was drafted in as the bad guys to interrogate us – and it's fair to say they adapted to their role playing with gusto. For eleven hours we were stripped naked, stood in stress positions, subjected to 'white noise' and had Rottweilers' peeing all over us. At the end we were let go in groups of three or four in a staged escape with only a map reference, a pair of boots and an all-in-one biological suit.

The S.A.S. played fair; gave us a head start and told us they'd better not catch us for the next nine days: Or else!

We met our 'Resistance' contact at the given grid reference – and he was something right out of the television comedy, 'Allo 'Allo: Not only was he dressed like a French onion seller, but he'd just been "pissing by" and thought we would, "Leek theese:" A map of the area we were to remain in for the nine days and a number of map references from where we'd be able to get food. "Don't get caught," he advised us as he pedalled away.

And we had no intention of letting that happen; not after just spending the worst eleven hours of our lives. One thing we agreed on right away: We'd go nowhere near the food drops, so we checked what we had between us to eek out the week or more. It didn't take long – everything had been taken from us, except for the fifty Mark note that each of us had managed to hide: And you don't want to know where.

150 Deutschmarks – about fifty quid: Enough to stop us starving – or to get some cigarettes and a beer or two in.

Next decision: Where are we going? The S.A.S. teams and their dogs were already after us. A quick decision needed: We weren't staying in the nominated exercise area – and just off the map was a small town which was bound to have a shop and no 'enemy' would think to look there.

A good plan: So we're off and running.

Unfortunately, as we approached the large village-cum-town, we made a mistake. We stole an axe out of a shed. I don't know why we did it, now: We can't really have been going to kill the search dogs? But, days later, details of the theft filtered back to our hunters allowing them to move their search area to just where we were.

Things were difficult enough already. Trips to the supermarket involved crawling along ditches then, dressed as we were in our stinking, and slime covered, green bio suits, making a dash across the main road. The local German population were marvellous: Bemused at first; then amused; then helpful in the extreme doing the shopping for us.

However, they weren't as good as the gentleman who found us in his back garden. Well, he didn't actually find us; it was his Alsatian, wet snout nuzzling our sleeping faces. The dog frightened us to death: We thought it belonged to the S.A.S. – only this one was as friendly as its master.

The German guy began by bringing out tea and biscuits on his best china, and when we told him we were pretending to be escaped prisoners of war, he laughed fit to bust: When he stopped: "Come tonight to my house. We have a drink."

That night, we drank so much of his beer it was thought best if we slept in his spare room. Next morning, we woke to a full breakfast being cooked for us – which was gratefully devoured.

Only one of our little group had a conscience: "We're supposed to be surviving," he argued.

"Quite right:" replied the German. "You go into my garden and survive until lunch: Eggs on toast….." he suggested.

Conscience thus satisfied, we survived until the eggs were ready; then survived until the roast dinner that evening. Then we drank – and slept in the spare room.

As a 'thank you' to the German, we taught his young son how to set traps for rabbits; even took him night fishing.

After the nine days of continual 'surviving' the German's hospitality, we walked back; the best fed survivors the army ever had. But we thought we'd better put on a bit of an act; so we began to stagger, holding our bellies; that sort of thing. Men ran toward us with water and plenty of slaps on the back.

The second in command comes across. He's really pleased with us. "There aren't many men who can outwit the S.A.S.," he says. "We're all very proud of you. A credit….."

The Officer Commanding wasn't so sure – he suspected we'd worked a flanker somehow, but couldn't prove it: But he did try. Immediately he caused mess tins to be produced; full to overflowing with army stew. And the grub kept on coming.

It was hard – we'd just eaten a full breakfast; then a packed lunch for the walk back – but we had to eat the stew: All of it: Plate after plate after plate:

And that was the hardest part of our time on the run.

N.B: We sent the German householder a squadron shield and a thank you letter: Unofficially of course.

A RED MOON

The wall was down. Hardly had the dust settled before we decided to go and have a look at East Germany; eight of us squaddies in two cars; XR3 injections with all the trimmings.

We'd no idea where to go, how to get there, or what we'd find. With so much P.P.P. [piss poor preparation,] it should come as no surprise that we achieved the maximum P.P.P. as a result. [Piss poor performance.]

We got lost in a town without a name which still had bomb damaged buildings from the Second World War. There must have been one hell of a fire-fight in the town when the Russians got here as the amount of bullet scarred frontages was phenomenal. It was as though nothing had been touched since 1945: Incredible.

And the Russian garrisons were still here; the soldiers pausing from their job of sweeping the barren, desolate streets to stare at these two powerful Westernized cars throbbing slowly passed. From the looks, there'd be no love lost with this particular bunch.

Colditz was a mental hospital – and about as welcoming as the Russkies. Then there was the pub we stopped at for a beer; only the place was full of the smell of blocked toilets and ice cold stares.

Time to liven things up: The cops only had Lada's: No chance of catching us, although to give them credit, they did set up a speed trap very quickly. Their problem, however, was that they didn't have radar guns like we have in the West. Here it was being done 1960's style – take a fixed point; [a bridge in this case,] and use a stopwatch to take a precise time to the next fixed point one-third of a mile ahead.

We were too fast.

But we gave them a fair go: Two more fly-passed's and we were ready for the finale: Off we went: Police aghast: Passed the Russian soldiers still showing not an ounce of humour between them. Not until we were out of town, were six bare backsides withdrawn from the open windows and decency restored.

The best moonee ever:

PUSHED TO THE LIMITS

It had taken a long time to get here – wherever here was: According to Scotty, my navigator who was armed to the teeth – and with three stripes, he got the map, - we were somewhere in the middle of Armagh: Bandit Country; and it was the height of 'The Troubles.'

We had no need to worry though, as all we had to do was follow the armoured Land Rover packed with troops and machine guns which doddled along fifty yards in front of us. It must have been frustrating for our bodyguards, as at every bend in the road they'd have to wait for us to catch up. Well; we were in a truck which weighed the best part of a hundred tons and with a road which went up and down in a never-ending, roller-coaster fashion, we needed every one of our eighteen gears.

Did I say there was no need to worry? Maybe not from the Provo's – but when the brakes went on the massive truck just over the brow of a steep hill, things got a bit worrisome.

We picked up speed: Faster and faster; the rear of the Land Rover began to fill the windscreen:

Then the engine blew up - which meant I couldn't use the gears to slow us down:

"Get ready to jump, Scotty," I said, trying to play it cool.

"Yeah: Right."

I had the reputation for being a bit of a joker, but I reckon the white face and the, "No – seriously," shook him. The passenger door was open in a flash.

"Hang-on," I cried! The escort had noticed their imminent demise and floored the accelerator. The Land Rover roared away from us; then stopped at the top of the next hill as if it was looking back like an animal which had just had a scare and need to check it out.

We charged up the hill; then began to slow perceptibly; but just before the crown, our monster truck began to roll back.

"Please don't let anything come up behind us: Please don't….." I prayed.

The truck got faster and faster – only now we were hurtling backwards, charging up the hill on the other side, slowing perceptibly; then forward.

And so gravity took its course: Up: Slow: Back: Fast: Down: Fast: Up: Slow; until we finish in the dip between the two hills.

With much relief, we drop the five feet to the ground, legs shaking. We may be more vulnerable to attack now, but the Land Rover was hurtling toward us, guns bristling. I knew someone would already be shouting for helicopter back-up.

Before the cigarettes were out, a lieutenant was approaching: Worse: A new lieutenant straight out of school, university and Sandhurst who knew everything there was to know about everything.

"We'll use the Foden recovery vehicle to give you a tow," he says.

"Eh….. No sir. You can't do that," I said.

"Yes I can."

"Eh…..Sorry sir: But you can't possibly tow this monster with a fifty ton recovery vehicle."

"We'll do it; don't you concern yourself, sapper."

"Tell him sergeant," I asked Scotty.

And he did; but it made not one jot of difference: Lobotomy Boy had made a decision.

The tow made it – to the first decline that is; before gravity took over. The monster truck picked up speed; picked-up the fifty-tonner; turned it on its side and pushed it through a hedge.

I handed a ciggy to Scotty. No words were necessary, but we couldn't help it: "Ooops!"

IT'S A KNOCKOUT

A new lad comes to join our section in Northern Ireland: A Welsh lad from the Head of the Valleys who could have dug out five tons of coal a shift with a pick-axe – if there'd been any pits left that is.

So, he's as strong as an ox, but as green as the hills he'd left behind when it came to soldiering: He was clueless. In fact, it would have been criminal to let him out to patrol the streets of the province; the hostile locals would have had him for breakfast.

A bit of extra tuition is called for:

In full kit, he leaves the barracks alone, weapon in hand. He's been told to patrol correctly to the front gate and he does okay to start with; weapon held low; turning every few steps he takes to check what is happening all about him. And the lads are quite pleased; perhaps he'll make the grade after all…..

However: It was a great pity he chose to turn about exactly where he did – and a greater pity he failed to notice the heavy boom falling across the road just outside the Guard Commander's office. It crashed down with a thump – landing right on top of his head. He was unconscious for days.

Taff was an unlucky lad. There was a curfew at 1.30 a.m. at the barracks, brought in to stop the squaddies spending the night with any local girls they'd met. This 'honey-trap' had led to several murders of unsuspecting, randy, security force personnel, so it was a good move. Only Taff was late back – not a woman, more twenty pints of Guinness and a curry. He was so drunk that he could hardly stand, but he wanted his bed and fortunately a mate of his was on guard duty, sneaking him through the gate. Unfortunately some workmen had dug an eight foot deep trench inside the camp and not marked it.

Taff is in, then down and out in the hole. He couldn't understand why he was unable to climb his way out, so he forgets bed and makes himself comfortable on the muddy bottom of the trench and falls asleep.

Next morning, he's found; still sleeping it off. Only he's broken his leg so badly, he's hospitalized for three months.

But that was Taff.

THE FALKLANDS: 1982

I suppose we can all remember the images of our troops, yomping across the barren wastes of the islands in the South Atlantic during the conflict with Argentina.

What didn't hit the television screens was the less heroic episode when twenty Royal Marines called a ten minute rest break. Their packs were so heavy, [110 lbs.] that they couldn't sit down because they'd never be able to stand up again; so they all rested the bottom of their rucksacks on a line of fence posts.

Within seconds, the rotten posts had given way, leaving twenty pairs of arms and legs thrashing about like upturned turtles.

*

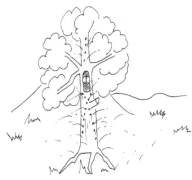

One unit is under attack from a sniper. The men hit the deck – a very wet and soggy, moorland deck.

"Where is he," shouts the sergeant?

No one has any idea.

"Jack: On your feet: Zigzag ten yards and hit the deck. Go!"

Jack's up and away running for his life.

Ping: Ping: The sniper gets off two shots before Jack disappears.

"Anyone see him," snaps the sergeant?

"No serge," came the reply from all around him.

"Jack: You'll have to do it again. Go!"

Jack's off: Zigzagging like a good 'un.

One shot: Missed.

"Anyone see him?"

"I think he's in that tree, sergeant," volunteers one guy.

"Don't be daft, lad. It's the only bloody tree for miles. He must be in the grass tufts somewhere: Jack."

Jack's off – probably saying to himself, "Why me," – but he makes it.

"Well done, lad," shouts the sergeant; then to the rest of the troop: "Any ideas?"

"He's definitely in that tree," says the first bloke; and this time two others agree with him.

"They can't be that stupid," says the sergeant to himself: But why not: "Fire on the tree," he calls out.

Two seconds later: "Cease fire!"

The sergeant stands up: "Let's hope they're all that bloody stupid."

Northern Ireland: We're working in the area where there is a village which is now known world wide because of its road sign: 'Sniper at work.'

It's fair to say the presence of British troops in this neck of the woods is not tolerated; frequent mortar shells land in the fortresses and if possible, the security forces prefer to travel by helicopter.

Only you can't helicopter in a hundred trucks – that delight is down to us in the Royal Engineers who are tasked to re-build a bombed-out fort.

FOOD FIGHT AT THE OK CORAL!

The convoy travels at night. 2 a.m. and the eighty-eight tonners are in low gear, revving their way through the villages. Even at that time of night, lights come on in the houses, front doors are opened and paint bombs, sticks, stones and abuse are all hurled at the troops by kids as young as five.

My co-driver, Freddie, wasn't in a good mood – and a whole lot of us owe our lives to him because of what he did next. He opened the 'Horror Box:' a container kept in the cab where mingin' sandwiches, black bananas, apple gowks and all the rest of the rubbish is stored – and begins to hurl the rotten fruit at the locals.

They aren't happy – especially when all the truck crews join in.

We arrive at our destination and set to work. Days later, the job is finished – only our locals don't want us to leave anymore. This is obvious because of the tens of thousands of nails, screws and three pointed, metal jacks that have been strewn across every road out of the fort.

There's no way you can drive the vehicles out, so I'm flown back to Antrim to collect a road sweeper machine. Back on site, the sweeper is attached to a Land Rover and our route out is swept. It meant a delay of twelve hours – and eleven and a half in, the Search Team finds a two thousand pound device waiting for us under a culvert drain.

If it hadn't been for Freddy's fruit, the locals wouldn't have delayed us with the nails

and what have you – and the culvert bomb wouldn't have been found.

Funny old world:

*

But we still had to get back.

Half way down the hill into the village, I felt a bumping sensation under our eighty-eight ton truck. We were still moving, but not everything felt just right with the Scammell.

"Did you feel….," I asked?

"Look at that," says Freddy at the same time. "Hope they aren't ours."

I looked - and saw – and couldn't quite believe: Two huge wheels had detached themselves from an axle, overtook us and headed down the hill picking up speed as they went. Now, each wheel weighed three hundred pounds, so it was a bit worrying for anyone 'out there' as there was nothing we could do.

At the bottom of the hill the road divided into two at a classic 'Y' junction: To the right lay a country road; to the left, the main street through the village.

Just like in the comic books, one wheel went right; the other left. They must have been travelling at thirty miles an hour at that stage.

The 'right' wheel ended up in a field half a mile away, having entered it through an open gate; the left one carried on down the High Street, missing every car; every obstruction; every house, until it murdered two garden gnomes and sunk itself into a garden pond.

Problem: Two wheels, each weighing three hundred pounds and each at either end of a hostile village.

The Decision: Keep the 'Horror Box' out of sight and maybe, just maybe, the locals wouldn't notice us…..

BITS AND PIECES

The Royal Engineer [Combat Support] boat crew were called out at 2 a.m: – something not universally popular with the two man crew: Stewy and Pete who were both known to like their beauty sleep.

But the call out had come from the Royal Ulster Constabulary: A body had been reported floating in the River Foyle outside of Londonderry.

They got there and launched the 'Free Derry Ferry' as their C.S.B. was nicknamed and out they went into the night. Their boat was all of twenty feet long and made of aluminium, so every lump and bump reverberated through the hull; but it was undoubtedly good enough for the job in hand.

Both Pete and Stewy were up the front; Pete at the steering wheel with his partner hanging over the bow, torch in one hand and skimming the light back and forth over the black and fast moving water. He knew what to do all right: He'd watched all the television documentaries about crocodile catching at night; you know; where the light plays on the croc's eyes. Only dead eyes don't shine.

It should come as no surprise, therefore, that the first time Stewy saw the body was when the bow gave it a nudge, rolling it onto its back. The head and face were horrendous; a mash of half-decomposed and half-eaten flesh with the eyes long gone.

Unfortunately, Stewy's face was only twelve inches above the water at that time and it all came as a bit of a shock. He threw himself backwards onto the floor of the boat, giving out a blood curdling scream. He gave Pete such a fright, that he automatically gunned the outboard.

The Combat Support Boat threw itself into a tight circle, travelling fast – and dragged the corpse under it. Bum-Bump; bum-bump, it went before Pete got the boat under control again and drew once more alongside the dishevelled bundle of clothes floating nearby.

Problem: The body no longer had its head: The propeller had seen to that; and try as they might; flashing the little torch this way and that, it was long gone.

'Ah well,' the lads thought, 'at least we'll get the rest to shore: Give the poor bloke a proper funeral.' Stewy grabbed for the corpse's jacket – and pulled. He'd managed to secure; then raise, the body until it was just a few inches below the gunwale, before Pete left the wheel and came to help. He grabbed at the torso and pulled – only his hand pierced the decomposing flesh and his arm plunged into the foul smelling gore; right up to the forearm.

"Agh," Pete screamed! Then promptly fell over backwards - onto Stewy.

"Agh," Stewy screamed as the smell of putrefaction filled the night air.

The body fell back into the water.

"Right," said Pete, getting the boat alongside again. "We'll tow it in," no doubt thinking of the clean-up job once the body hit the deck.

Stewy was all for it, grabbed the deceased's legs; tied them tightly together above the ankles and lashed them to the back of the boat on a long line. They were off – pleased with themselves at resolving a tricky problem and looking forward to an early return to bed.

Stewy opened up the throttle; [his turn to be captain] and headed towards the gaggle of cops on the far shore. In their relief, or excitement, the two man crew failed to notice that, because of their speed, the body was now surfing; skimming the surface of the river behind them; bumping over the wake the boat was leaving.

Then disaster for Pete: He'd taken to standing in the front of the boat, enjoying the exhilaration of the moment; the speed; the air hurtling passed his face: Until he hit the mosquito cloud, that is. He reacted to the impact of a million insects being smashed into his face and arms by brushing them away with the back of his hand: Only it was the hand which had been plunged into the body's innermost cavities. He vomited his was back to the shore; the foulness entrenched in his huge, Mexican moustache.

"Where's the head," demanded the R.U.C. police inspector?

Stewy answered as Pete was still puking. "No head when we arrived there, sir. Sorry and all that. We did look."

"Blast," the policeman exclaimed! "It'll be hard to identify without the dental records. Let's hope we can get some fingerprints."

Stewy kept pulling at the rope and the bundle of clothes sped easily to the shore: Too easily. All that was left of the body was the two lower legs and feet – the bound bits: The rest was long gone in the water ski run.

The words of the R.U.C. man were not fit for human consumption; but not half as harmful as the consequences for Pete: He only stopped vomiting when he'd shaved off his prized moustache.

STANDING ON CEREMONY

The guardsman had his orders: It might be London in the middle of summer with eager tourists thronging every street, but the royals were in town and that meant everyone had to be one their toes.

The orders: No one is to step over THAT painted white line. If they do; deal with it.

An American lady comes up to the guardsman and starts taking his picture. And that's all right. She even manoeuvres herself so that the very large notice: 'DO NOT CROSS,' doesn't spoil the shot.

Not satisfied with her efforts, she then puts a foot over the white line: THAT white line. The guardsman comes to attention: "Step back from the line," he orders, and she does so.

He returns to the 'stand at ease' position; rifle butt on the ground and bayonet at a 45 degree angle: All very proper and correct.

The American woman thinks this is all very unusual; so she does it again: Foot over the line: Same result.

"Are you getting this guy, honeykins?" she drawls to her husband who has one eye stuck in the view finder of a video camera. To make sure he's 'got it,' she steps fully over the line, posing by the sign and the guardsman.

The guardsman comes to attention; only this time he adopts the 'challenge' position where the rifle and bayonet are in front of him – and pointing at the portly American lady. "Step back over the line," he says, matter-of-factly.

She's agog: "Did you see that honey," she asks as she steps back?

The guardsman returns to the 'at ease' position.

'Just once more,' the lady thinks to herself: 'It's good fun, this.' She jumps over the line.

The guard's rifle is coming up.

"Da-da;" she sing-songs: Then: "Agh!" she screams at the top of her voice whilst looking disbelievingly at the bayonet stuck in her thigh.

"Step back over the line….: Please," the soldier adds with a smile.

Cyril was the nicest man you could ever meet. He was a practising Christian and so timid that he'd never plucked up the courage to tell his wife that he didn't like bananas: Never had and never would – even though she had been putting one in his lunch box every day for the last fifteen years.

At the time I was working out of the vehicle office in a Royal Engineers depot near London, and Cyril was one of my civvy drivers. As such, he had a lot of contact with car company representatives who would visit us practically every day; but this could only happen to Cyril:

An elderly lady walks in to our office and he immediately assumes she's from one of the hire companies. I wasn't so sure; she's a bit old and a bit scruffy – rep's usually wear suits, but I'm on the phone and have four fingers stuck in various pages in a complicated contract, so it's up to Cyril.

He invites her to sit and asks her what he can do for her, whereupon she puts her head in her hands and starts to cry. The tears are flowing.

"Are you all right?" Cyril asks, very concerned by now. But all she does is rachet up the noise and the tears. There's even stuff pouring out of her nose which she's wiping on her coat sleeve.

"Do you want a banana?" he asks, no doubt hoping to get rid of his unwanted lunch, but when that doesn't work, he puts his arm around her. "Don't upset yourself, love."

I'm beginning to think:'Nutter:' Not that I'm quick on the uptake – but you latch onto these things when first the jumper; then a tee-shirt; a bra; jeans; panties; all come zinging across the room. She's crying and carrying-on: Cyril is squirming in the corner: He's never seen anything like it – and the rest of us head for the door.

Behind us, the naked woman is rushing about the office, knocking phones and blotters and paperwork trays; anything and everything, onto the floor. She's even seen stomping Cyril's banana to mush.

Poor Cyril: He can't get passed her, so he's cringing in the corner, no doubt hoping he won't go the same way as the fruit.

The squishy banana did it: It was stuck between her toes and so she decided she needed to clean up and headed for the sink in the corner - where the lads kept a huge jar of green, skin cleanser; the stuff that removes oil and grease from your hands. The whole jar is used as she covers herself from head to toe in a green gunge.

Now; not only do I have a naked woman in my office; I have a naked green woman.

An officer arrives at the double: "What's this I hear about you having trouble with a sixty year old lady?" You could hear the sneer in his voice.

Without a word, I open the outer door: The green goddess appears out of the darkened recesses. "Oh! Carry on then corporal:" And he leaves.

It takes an hour, but good old Cyril eventually manages to talk her into wearing a boiler suit – a combat green boiler suit which matched her face, hair and hands perfectly. As she was loaded into the ambulance which eventually arrived, I couldn't help but think that her new appearance would make the job of the psychiatrist a whole lot easier.

THE THUNDERBOX

This is a story of British ingenuity versus the methodical approach of our German allies.

I can't say I blame the Germans for changing the type of latrine provided on exercise: One look at the blue-Elsen-dyed British soldiers, who'd suffered practical jokes whilst going to the loo, was enough of an incentive to change. For some reason, they didn't want their soldiers to look like the ancient, woad covered, warriors who faced down the Roman Empire.

Instead of the Elsen cubicles, they opted for a giant hole in the ground, with individual cubicles set around the edge. A dry toilet akin to the Aussie bush toilets, 'The Long Drop.'

"What are you doing," I asked? Not an unusual question in the circumstances as Terry, a freckled-faced, ginger-haired, Geordie, had his head and shoulders down a German lavatory pan.

"Just lookin,'" he replied innocently, pulling himself back in from outside, "to see where to chuck these."

The three thunder-flashes he'd tied together would hurl the contents of the giant midden thirty feet into the air.

The soldiers may not be turned blue – but.....

VERTICAL LIMITS

Digger, as you already know, was a big lad who earned his nickname because a normal sized shovel would simply disappear in his hands. And give him his due, he could dig.

But Digger was accident prone. He'd clean his rifle with a bullet up the spout, expressing shock – horror when holes appeared in the barrack walls, or would frown in incomprehension when the delivery driver starts jumping up and down because two bullet holes have just made a mess of the back doors of his van.

So, when we go to the grenade pit for training, we are all on edge.

The procedures there are very strict; no messing about is tolerated – you can get hurt here. The trouble with procedures is that they have to be talked through and the more procedures; like walking with the grenade in a hand on the end of an outstretched arm, the more bewildering it becomes to the more mentally challenged – like Digger.

We're behind the blast wall when the instructor leads him away to throw his grenade. The pin came out; only Digger was so worried by all the explanations, that he threw it a long, long way: All his strength went into it: Only it went straight up to the heavens – not out into the sandy pit.

Luckily, the grenade went so high, that they had time to run, making it to our distant blast wall before the air burst.

We could have done without the puncture, and as the whole convoy ground to a halt, the looks of exasperation gave way to those of resignation. Nothing much else could go wrong.

And it's funny how things do go wrong in direct proportion to how tired you are. Tired: We were beyond tired. It was over three days since we'd slept and I, for one, had experienced a whole battalion of First World War soldiers marching toward us, whistling: Then carried on right through our ranks to disappear into thin air: That's tired. True: We weren't far from Ypres; 'Vipers' as my Northumbrian pitmen forebears called it – so maybe the ghosts were 'real.'

What was real, was the puncture: Back offside tyre: So what, I hear you say? – But when it's an army Scammell loaded with bridge building equipment weighing the best part of one hundred tons: Well; we could do without it.

The whole vehicle had sagged to the right; the camber of the road making the angles a whole lot worse; certainly making it more difficult if not downright dangerous.

Despite our bone-weariness, our troop commander came up with a good idea. It might just be a faulty tyre valve. If so, we could whip in a replacement; re-inflate the thing and be off.

I doubted it – but it was worth a try: Anything to avoid having to unload. That would take forever.   "Go get a valve and bung it in," he ordered a couple of guys standing nearby sharing a fag and looking dejected.

Off they went – and returned a few minutes later; triumphant; replacement valve in hand and showing it proudly to the troop commander.

I know they were tired – but did they have to take the blessed thing from the front offside tyre?

With an unnaturally loud hissing sound breaking the unbelieving silence, the huge lorry tilted to the right even more; then tilted again…..

Now Geordie was the most unlikely type of person to ever wear the Queen's uniform. His black hair was always too long; his thick moustache never trimmed and gave him the air of a Mexican bandit. The pock-marked face and the ever present shadow of facial hair made him a nightmare to be on parade with as no matter how smart the creases in his uniform, how polished his cap, belt buckle and buttons; he looked a mess.

However, he was a good soldier and after several mundane years as a Sapper in the Engineers, Geordie saw a chance for a bit of excitement. A notice had been pinned up outside the mess: "Blah-blah…..Undercover work…..blah-blah…..Special forces….."

So Geordie applies and in due course the memo arrives directing him to attend for interview. An N.B. at the bottom directed: 'Wear appropriate dress.'

The appointed day arrives and Geordie turns up – only to be confronted by an ante-room full of soldiers waiting to be interviewed: And every one of them was immaculately

dressed in new suits, ties and polished shoes. With their fresh haircuts, each looked pristine and clean and a credit to their regiments, their families and themselves.

Geordie may have been from a council estate in the west end of Newcastle upon Tyne – a place affectionately known as the 'Wild West' – but even he was wondering if he'd messed his chances up before he'd even been interviewed.

The reason: He looked down at his wet and dirty, motor cycle leathers; his scuffed motor cycle boots – and then at the helmet he was swinging in one hand. Now nervous, he was beginning to play with the bits of hair which were hanging over his ears.

It took a couple of seconds; then his worst fears came true as the R.S.M. in charge of the interviewees marched over. He peered at this apparition that had appeared before him; that had dared enter his sanctuary looking like…..."Like a turd," [In his own words.]

Geordie said nothing – he was too experienced to challenge an R.S.M. in full flow – just coming to attention.

"It says here," said the Regimental Sergeant Major, waving the joining instructions in Geordie's face: "To dress appropriately."

"But I did, sir," he replied. "I came on my motor cycle."

That fair wound the senior man up. 'In all his thirty years, no one had ever attended for interview looking like a…..'

He never got to finish his sentence, as a lieutenant opened the interview room door. Geordie suspected [later] that the officer must have been watching it all through a hidden camera or something, because his timing was perfect.

"Thank you, Regimental Sergeant Major: You, young man," the officer said beckoning Geordie with a crooked finger: "With me."

Geordie got the job: The only one.

CHIEF BIG TIM

We'd been on exercise in Canada. For three months we'd been chasing about the never-ending plains of Saskatchewan dodging charging battle tanks and low flying helicopters, but now all that was coming to an end. Two weeks leave – but out here!

Fortunately, our troop leader was a good guy and organized a holiday for us – on Tim's ranch. And Tim was only too pleased to see us, initially. Well, who wouldn't be happy to have twenty self-sufficient squaddies turn up on your property to do anything that needed doing: In exchange for ten days work, we'd get a three day trek on his horses out into the foothills of the Rockies: A great way to get all your wood chopped ready for winter; all your neglected fences put to rights.

Only Tim was in for a shock. It takes a bit to shock into silence a Native American Indian who was as big as the rodeo bulls he rode for fun. This guy was massive. But he was stunned into silence when he visited our encampment. Our tents were up, camp fire lit, grub sizzling away in pans; a scene of perfect happy campers. Only he couldn't quite believe his eyes – our beer had a tent of all its own: Boxes of the stuff packed tight from end to end.

"Get one thing straight," he ordered. "If you so much as go near any of my horses when you're pissed, I'll kill you."

That put a bit of a damper on the party – he wasn't joking. And I don't suppose this man-mountain would have needed the rifle he carried around with him to see all twenty of us off.

It was a bit subdued for a while after he left, but obviously he had a conscience: He was back with a genuine Peace-pipe: I kid you not.

"We'll share a pipe," he said, then spent an awful long time filling the bowl whilst we sat cross-legged around the camp fire. I don't know what he put in the pipe, but we were all as mellow as mellow can be as it was passed from hand to hand on the first circle: Second time around the circle and we're deliriously happy: Third: Unconscious. Who needs beer!

The ten days work was over: Time for the wilderness trek. Much excitement as the expedition sorted itself out – but for sure; these horses knew we were all novices and decided to exercise their sense of humour.

We were off. No charging about like John Wayne: Not on these animals. They plodded in line, heads drooped as though it was all too much – and this jaunt wasn't on their horsy social calendar.

When they got fed up of walking in line, they'd bite; then take off – fast; heading for the trees: Killer horses trying their best to dislodge their learner-drivers: Under low branches; skimming passed tree trunks – so close the riders should have lost legs or heads.

Then Tim or one of his riders would be there; whipping the horses back into line: Plod-plod – until the stallions began showing an undue interest in the female of the species: Hang on tight and shout for Chief Tim.

Back in line: And so it went on – and on – until we were beyond saddle sore.

Eventually it was time to turn the horses for home. Our plodders turned immediately into race horses. They were gone like the wind; their human charges hanging on for grim death: Hanging onto straining and sweating horsy necks; slipping saddles; dangling reins: One of our blokes even jumped for an overhead branch, and hung there: Anything was better than the certain death his horse had in store for him.

It may have taken two days to trek out; it took but four hours to get back to the ranch.

It's time for yet another B.F.T. [Basic Fitness Test.] For us operating in Northern Ireland there is no public road to run on; no scenic paths – just two-and-a-half times around the hangers on the base behind high security fences.

CHEATS NEVER PROSPER

Taking the test are two lads who are always overweight. If they'd drink less beer and eat fewer chips, they might be able to run faster and so make their compulsory times for the distance to be covered. But as they don't work at their fitness, they have to resort to more and more extraordinary methods to make sure they pass the B.F.T.

One ruse is to cut through the hangers and re-join the group that have slogged all the way around it. Another: To stop by whatever piece of machinery is available; pretend to tie a shoe lace; then hide there until the rest of their colleagues come round on the next circuit. In that way they miss a complete lap.

And so they always pass – and pass well. Their times are up there with the best.

And that was okay – until the new sergeant major turned up. This bloke was really keen on cross country running and wherever he'd been stationed he'd organized a team and entered it in whatever local, sometimes national, events that were going on.

He makes his selection for his team from our regiment – only as he doesn't know anyone, it has to be based on the completed time sheets handed in after each fitness test. The two overweight soldiers are selected to represent the army at a forthcoming athletics meet.

They can't believe it. Mind you, the sergeant major couldn't believe it either when they trailed in last; a full hour behind everyone else.

DIGIT McGEE

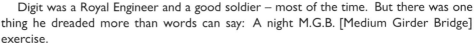

Digit was a Royal Engineer and a good soldier – most of the time. But there was one thing he dreaded more than words can say: A night M.G.B. [Medium Girder Bridge] exercise.

A good team can throw a bridge over a river within two hours – but that was unlikely if Digit was involved. He'd won his nickname by managing to sever three fingers in a roller pedestal used for pushing the bridge over the obstacle and on one occasion when he was on the flat bed of a lorry trailer, he'd somehow managed to strap his foot to the equipment on a pallet. When the "Tea up" call came, he turned and jumped from the truck; only the strapping wouldn't let him go. From twenty yards away, we could hear the ankle snap – just like a rifle shot.

But fair-do's: Digit liked the army life and so was determined to put up with the occasional downside - like when he lost his fingers. It could have put him off forever, but didn't. It happened like this: The three fingers had gone, blood everywhere and he's rushed to the Q.M.S.I. who's enjoying a cup of tea in his office. Now the Q.M.S.I. is hard; I mean HARD. Nearly 20 years of humping steel girders meant his body was like iron and he'd been everywhere; done and seen everything.

"You two - OUT!" he ordered Digit's helpers and when they'd gone asked, "Where are your fingers?" He was oblivious to the spurting blood.

"Dunno, sir."

"They're on my bridge, aren't they? I know they are. Get out of my office and get your **** body parts off MY **** bridge."

Digit was as white as a sheet by now, loss of blood and all that, so plucked up some courage. "When I find my fingers sir, can I have an ambulance then?" he pleaded.

"Just get your property off my bridge, then we'll see."

His first few days back with us from hospital and its bridge building again. The weeks away hadn't made him any fitter: In fact, he's slow; something spotted by the corporal who teamed him up with a super-fit partner when it came to laying the bridge decking; the final job. It may have been done with the best of intentions — but it was a wrong move by the corporal.

Now; you start laying the decking on the bridge from the farthest point; two men holding each piece between them; running out; dropping it into place; then returning for the next: A bit like a bean-bag race on a school sports day — but requiring muscles.

Digit and his super-fit partner are off and running. Within seconds, the faster man is in front; the angle of the decking going from 180 degrees to near vertical which made Digit run in the centre of the unmade bridge: The piece which hadn't been filled in.

And Digit finds the hole; disappearing into the blackness with the decking following him in short order. He lands with his midriff right on the criss-cross, metal sway braces; executes a perfect 360 degree vault as good as anything you'd see in the gym halls of the Olympic Games, and 'dismounts' into the torrent below.

The corporal who tried to do him a favour is on the river bank waiting as the slime monster crawls out on all fours, spluttering and splurting.

"Stand up you horrible little man," the corporal orders: "Turn round:" And as a breathless Digit does so, the N.C.O. takes him by the collar and trouser belt and throws him back in. "Don't you dare come out of there without my ** decking."

We're in a Royal Engineer depot in Germany and things are pretty quiet for a change — or at least would have been if it wasn't for a new lieutenant who was intent on running us about for no real reason. Only, for now, he's off duty and all was quiet.

The lieutenant was one of these young men who knew it all; was always immaculately groomed and you just knew that when he was back in the U.K., the lady on his arm would be called Penelope or Lucinda who thought a hard day's work was riding a polo pony: 'Lord Flash Heart:' You get the idea: Image was all to our young man and so he'd adopted one of the army's very new motor cycles as his very own: State of the art stuff: [Not!]

Of course, he couldn't help but show it off and then, when he invited comments, we'd try and put him out of his stride: 'Bad reputation:' 'The thing-a-me-bit is too experimental:' 'Keep it below 120 k.p.h. or…..'

He's back from leave, roaring around the yard again, swinging the bike round in real show-off fashion. "Fill it up, Bungle," he says to a sapper, sitting having a smoke.

Now you would think that even a lieutenant would guess that something may be

behind calling a soldier, 'Bungle.' Not a bit of it.

So Bungle heads to the dual fuel pod and fills the motor cycle up, whilst the officer combs his hair and tells us about the speeds he'd managed up the autobahn.

Bungles back; lethargically dropping onto the bench beside me.

The lieutenant gets ready to leave; helmet on; gloves on - and he's away across the yard on his bike; engine screaming as he pulls a 'wheelie.' He'd only travelled thirty yards when the engine on the motor cycle blew up in spectacular fashion: Blue cloying smoke filled the air.

"What did you put in it?" I asked, just knowing the answer.

"It's diesel ain't it?"

"No, Bungle, it's petrol."

"Oh: Ah well!"

The officer is fast approaching; a bemused look on his face. "I don't understand it," he said, near to tears.

"Told you; these types of bikes, sir. Unproven; that's what they are," I explained, covering up for Bungle.

"Yes they are, corporal. I'll speak to you about which one to buy before I take the plunge next time."

"Any time, sir."

I don't think he ever cottoned-on about Bungle's bungle.

*

Time improves most officers: They mellow; they learn; they begin to trust their men, but our young motor cycle fanatic wasn't one of them. He was too fond of his hair and shower accessories – and it just so happens, it was Bungle again.

The lieutenant gave him the job of stock taking: A bad job that never seems to go right. But to make matters worse, this was January in Germany and it was bitterly cold. And there wasn't any heat in the store room where Bungle found himself.

The lack of heat didn't sit well with the sapper, especially when the officer retired to his office warmed by a coal-fired pot bellied stove. Bungle's working himself up into a silent fury as he counted engine parts, wondering just how he could get his own back: He didn't have long to wait.

The lieutenant was stuck for something to do – so he decides on a fire drill without telling anyone. He activates the alarm and heads outside to watch the men clearing the building and assembling in the designated areas.

Only Bungle's not there.

"Come with me, corporal," orders the officer, and the two of us head back into the building, only to find Bungle is the lieutenant's office with an empty fire bucket in his hand.

"Didn't you hear the fire alarm," the officer demanded in a raised voice?

"Yes, sir," replies Bungle, coming to attention with a certain amount of jingling from the metal bucket.

"Then why didn't you obey Standing Orders?"

"Did, sir," came the reply.

It wasn't what the officer expected to hear – but really he shouldn't have asked.

Bungle directed the lieutenant's attention to the 'What to do in the event of fire,' plastic card stuck on the wall, before reeling off what he'd memorized:

"Identify the seat of fire
Shout fire three times
Put out fire or
If not possible; evacuate.

I did all that, sir. There was only one fire – yours: So I shouted, 'Fire-Fire-Fire' and put it out."

WAIT-ER MINUTE

One Christmas our Regimental Sergeant Major made a mistake: He ordered Walter, a sapper with twenty two years service nearly completed and who'd never been promoted, to act as a waiter for the officers and their ladies at the formal mess night celebrating the festive season.

Now Wally only had a couple of months left before he was compulsorily retired, so he wasn't best pleased to have this duty dumped on him. To show his displeasure, he turns up without being shaved and without ironing a single piece of kit.

However, he was already working the tables, rubbing shoulders with the officers in their 'monkey suits' and their ladies in their expensive designer gowns, before the R.S.M. sees him.

By the time the first two courses had been cleared, Wally was up to the back teeth with it all: He'd had enough. Hands full of the sweet course, he kicks open the double doors from the kitchen so hard that they smash back against the wall; and if that wasn't enough to get their attention, shouts at the top of his voice, "Put yer hands up if yer want a puddin'."

And six officers did before the R.S.M. grabbed him by the collar and 'helped' him out.

My driving instructor would have been proud of me – I think.

For my undercover job in Northern Ireland during 'The Troubles,' I needed to learn to drive all over again: No 'L' plates necessary – just the ability to get out of I.R.A. ambushes by doing all sorts of exciting things with our beat-up, super-charged, armour-plated, Fords and Vauxhalls or whatever else had been supplied in the belief they'd blend in with their surroundings.

HEDGING YOUR
BET

Not that they 'blended' for very long; not in such close-knit communities, so the motors were changed regularly. However, no one in the Top Brass ever seemed to be able to resolve the conundrum: That ANY motor vehicle which wasn't known to belong, automatically came under immediate suspicion by the terrorist sympathisers – and I guess that's what happened to me.

I'm travelling the by-ways of Armagh; Bandit Country, and although the lanes were narrow with hedges on either side, I was confident in my own abilities. After all, the instructor back in Hampshire was really pleased with his prize pupil: Me. I could spin the car on a sixpence, heading back in the same direction I'd come from without losing speed – well nearly. I could reverse like a maniac whilst shooting through windows: I could leap tall buildings – when you're young you can do that sort of thing.

But all that was as naught, when the pressure really came on. As I reach the brow of a small hill, I can see into the 'T' junction a quarter of a mile away: And there were two cars; one parked on either side of the 'T.'

The whole situation yelled, 'Ambush,' – and that's when your training is supposed to take over. I yank on the handbrake, spinning the wheel as I did so – only I'm no longer on a disused airfield, I'm in a narrow lane and now stuck broadside across it; front and back wheels in the bottoms of the hedges.

Panic: I gun the engine, giving it all the power it can muster. The car shoots forward: I'm turning the steering wheel to the right: Lots of noise and smoke and branches and leaves as a full fifteen yards of hedge is torn out by its roots.

I'm away: The farmer might not be happy; the local council may not be happy – and I'm not even sure my driving instructor would have been too impressed.

But why should I care: I'm away; ignoring the puncture, the smashed headlights; the half tree stuck in the windscreen and an exhaust that sounds like the fog horn of the Q.E.2. It might be noisy and I might have a bit of paperwork to do – but I'm away.

WOLFGANG THE MAGICIAN

We never knew how Wolfgang did it: A secure area in Germany; a tactical exercise in full flow. Helicopters are flying low; battle tanks are charging about every which way, churning up the ground into a quagmire out of which many a Land Rover and armoured car are being hauled: Smoke from artillery shells fills the air – and there's Wolfgang again.

The squaddies cheer, running from their foxholes; vehicles grind to a halt as the crews disembark to join the rush: "Wolfgang's here!"

The cry is on everyone's lips as we pursue the tinkling chimes of his ice cream van…..

THE DEPARTURE

I'm standing at one of those greasy mobile canteen things enjoying a cup of coffee and feeling like a million dollars. I'm doing the job I love; only I'm now in scruffy jeans and black leather jacket with a pistol stuck down in the small of my back body-guarding a colonel who's the brains behind something I don't understand, or could care less about.

It's my job to keep him safe — and this area is knee-deep in terrorists: Still, the coffee was good; spoiled only by the outbreak of small arms fire: Not too close, but close enough for me to find my firearm and the colonel.

Another spattering of gun fire.

"Shall we go and have a look," asks the boss? He was keen; I'll give him that and not many above lieutenant ask you what you think.

I nod: Why not: It could be one of our blokes in trouble: Might even be me tomorrow.

We'd got to the corner, a mere thirty yards away, when we were confronted by fifty Royal Marines. They were armed with everything you could think of — except tanks: Machine guns; side arms; combat knives between their teeth — that sort of thing. And they were running straight for us: Fast. Now these guys are fit — but they're sweating buckets: A long run then.

They pound passed.

"I wouldn't go down there, sir," one of them panted, recognizing the colonel: And was gone.

I looked at the boss too — then both of us looked at my tiny little pistol. Without a word, we were off after the marines. If they were departing; not even stopping at the tea van — then it must be serious:

It was a long run but worth it: The bomb was a big 'un.

WHERE ARE WE?

We were shattered. For days we'd been working to repair bomb blast damage to a R.U.C. police station; and now it was over.

Not long now and we'd be off. The helicopters would be here as and when — so we waited, happily stretched out in the summer sunshine, strewn along the grassy embankment like so many discarded toy soldiers. There we were; fag in one hand and soaking up the rays: At peace with the world.

Wokka-wokka: Wokka-wokka: The noise broke the silence.

"'Copter's have made good time, Scotty," I said.

"Yeh: Be off in a minute," he replied, pushing himself up with his elbows and peering over the embankment.

Wokka-wokka: Wokka-wokka: The sound came again.

"Can't see them though," he says, lying back down.

Wokka-wokka:

"Best get our kit together, lads," Scotty shouts after a few seconds. Being the corporal, he liked to do N.C.O. type things.

We start to rummage about.

Wokka-wokka-wokka.

Just then, all the radio's burst into life: Vehicle radios; back-up comms; everything: All lit up; going crazy, the operators talking over one another. "Contact: Contact:" someone was screaming down the airwaves.

Wokka-wokka.

"What are they saying," asks one of the blokes?

Wokka.....

"There's a contact somewhere....." We were all listening now.

"Contact: Rosslea: Contact: Rosslea:" The radio's are screaming.

"Where are we again," I ask Scotty?

He turns and points at the notice board outside the police station: Rosslea.

Wokka-wokka-wokka.

We dived for cover. The 'wokka's' were not helicopter noises – more fifty calibre machine gun bullets being fired at us from the back of a Land Rover about a kilometre away.

You'd think we'd know the difference.

TRUCK OFF

Doug was the Motor Transport Sergeant at Hameln in Germany. He'd been working under constant strain for two years now, trying to keep the old and unreliable fleet of ten tonners on the road. Things had got so bad, that his mechanics were having to cannibalize two trucks just to keep one running. And with the ever growing commitments for the army, he was just about at the end of his tether: His twenty two years couldn't come soon enough: Only eight more to go.

Then deliverance! A whole fleet of brand new trucks were waiting for us at the docks in Antwerp. Doug was beside himself with joy as he waved all his drivers off to do the collection run.

At the docks, things didn't go according to plan. Geordie opened his driver's door – just as another truck rumbled passed. The door was taken clean-off: A piece of less than text book reversing – and the front of a ten tonner, with only two miles on the clock; crumpled alarmingly.

But eventually the huge convoy arrived back at base. Sergeant Doug is there at the gate waving at each soldier as they drive through the gates: "Hi, Scouse: Hi, Jock: Hi, Pete: Hi George:"

His mouth fell open; words failed him as Geordie's truck – number five in line – drove passed him. "Good afternoon, sergeant," Geordie spoken nicely – through the open space where a door should have been.

Next in line passed without comment – but Doug was worrying now; no doubt remembering the old adage that nothing is squaddy proof.

Then came the crumpled truck – now on tow. Poor Doug: His happiest day is in ruins. He's near to tears; head in hands and staring at the ground as the rest of the convoy rumbles in.

Eventually there's silence and he wanders off: In his distress, he's lost count and there's one truck short. It would have been too cruel to tell him of its fate: Not on his happiest day.

THE BABY SITTERS

The Officer Commanding must have been desperate for a baby sitter – because he asked Kev and me.

We arrive, each carrying a 'yellow handbag' as we called the packs of beer; something to pass the time. We find the O.C. and his wife all dolled-up; they'd been looking forward to this night for ages. The kids were asleep in bed upstairs; we could order in a pizza; they'd even got a crate of beer for us to go along with the pile of hired videos. Very organized was our top man.

We drank all our beer – then his. We ordered and ate the pizza; then a Chinese, before falling over unconscious in front of the television.

It was 3 a.m. when they got home to find two drunken squaddies laid out in their front room amongst piles of discarded fast food packages and beer cans. I still don't know how many kids they had – but they must have counted them at some stage as all was correct. We were roused and sent off into the night.

A few days later our photographs appear on the squadron notice board: Photo's of two sprawling drunks amongst a devastated front room under the caption:

'Caution: Do not allow these men to baby-sit your children.'

THE BEST BREW EVER

Down on the border, where Northern Ireland meets the Republic, is a tiny ford across a tiny stream. Only this microscopic speck of territory has taken on a significance out of all proportion to its size.

The reason: It's an I.R.A. crossing point: A way to get arms, men and material across the border – and an escape route after the deed had been done.

The solution: Send in the Royal Engineers who would block the crossing point and so deny the enemy that use of space.

It sounds good on paper, but the area is so hostile; so dangerous, that the army sappers have to work under the cover of darkness. And that's okay – only it gets a bit disheartening when you return to work the following night to find most of what you'd done; undone.

We work and work; two steps forward and one step back; night after night, until the end of the job is in sight. The people with pips and scrambled egg on their shoulders are really pleased: Huge concrete blocks by the stream will do the job just fine.

Last night on site and we arrive. For some reason, no boss-men turn up and everything on site seems in order: Only that fact is strange in itself: But what the hell – we'd be gone by morning. With no 'brass' around, within five minutes we all slope off for a brew and a fag before getting down to it.

The kettle had hardly boiled before; 'B-O-O-M!' The explosion was big enough to rattle the fillings in your teeth and jump the whistling kettle off the camping gas. It rained pieces of concrete blocks for what seemed like ages.

The kettle is restored and another fag is called for: May as well take our time, we were going to be here for weeks. It wasn't until we were half way down the second brew that someone wised up. The Provo's must have been watching since we'd started the job; timing our arrival; noting our routines – then planting the bomb to cause maximum casualties.

But the one thing they hadn't counted on: No bosses, always equals a brew before the working day starts.

We all agreed: It was the best cuppa we'd ever had.

P.S. We were okay, but the Irish Army suffered five casualties that day.

ONCE UPON A TIME ....

Once upon a time, there was a dog; a very, very big dog: A brutish thing, large enough and fierce enough to face down a lion or two. And if that wasn't enough, it barked incessantly twenty four hours a day, frequently hurling itself at the wire mesh fence which surrounded the compound of its master's transport business. The perfect guard dog who'd only ever answer to its owner.

Now the owner was an I.R.A. sympathizer, with his transport yard right next to the place where some British marines set up camp.

I did say the dog took notice of its owner: Perhaps I should say 'sometimes.' Or maybe the Brit-hating Irish guy had learned his dog some perverse commands: 'Leave,' surely must have meant 'bite the so and so's,' as every time a patrol went passed the yard, the dog would come hurtling out to attack the soldiers. The more the owner shouted; the more blokes the dog bit.

This went on day after day – several times a day – for three months. And when the brute wasn't 'leaving,' it was barking as if determined no one would ever get any sleep.

Last day of the marines' deployment: Helicopters had come to collect them; jinking their way in to avoid being shot at. The guys were going home, but decided they really couldn't live any longer without the barking and biting. It was now so much part of their lives, it would be unthinkable to leave the Lion-dog behind.

So, one marine was sent out to act as a decoy – or dummy – and sure enough, the dog attacked. As it tried to eat the unfortunate soldier, several other marines came out of hiding and grappled it to the floor. Within seconds, its jaws were taped, and with a harness securing all four limbs, they legged-it to the helicopter with their prize.

At this point, legend takes over: The I.R.A. sympathizer would allege his dog plummeted from several thousand feet to disappear in the nearby lough forever: The marines would deny all knowledge of the dog – officially; but over drinks they'd tell the yarn over and over again. And with each telling, the story grew.

Lion-dog's jaws were so strong, that the leather muzzle couldn't hold it. Once the jaws were free, its huge incisors – the size of a Great White Sharks – undid the body harness; before it stood on its hind legs, saluted and [because its love for its owner was so great,] executed a perfect dive out through the open doorway of the helicopter shouting, 'Long live the Pope' as it went.

GUN CRIME

Scotland in summer and the midges are out in force. Still, it'll take a good 'un to get us as we're in full NBC kit, complete with masks. However, we are tired; really tired, after being run ragged over the Western Highlands, so it came as no surprise that during a ten minute halt, we all start to drop off to sleep.

But I'm not entirely stupid. I've met this particular officer before – so before allowing sleep to overtake me, I tie my rifle to my hand. It only felt like seconds, but we were all brought back to reality by a couple of thunder-flashes exploding amongst us.

The officer wasn't a happy man. Everyone's weapon – except mine – was stacked up in the middle of the clearing. He didn't half lay it on the line: A real tongue-lashing followed by a two mile run in full 'Noddy' kit. It's nearly impossible to take in enough air when you're breathing through the filters in the mask; so a match box comes in handy. Stick the match box below your chin and you get a bit of air in that way. Only with the air; come the midges.

We were in a state, totally exhausted and now with faces bitten to hell and back. We weren't happy.

Now, next day: What should we see but the officer standing in some bushes over a hundred yards away: And on the bonnet of his Land Rover – all unattended and alone, was his personal weapon: A sub machine gun.

And he wasn't looking.

And no one else was looking:

So…..

It took him hours to find it: What do they say about sympathy? If you are looking for it, try somewhere between 'shit' and 'syphilis' in the dictionary.

THE MINI-MAN

It's Bosnia and the civil war there is just about over.

The force under the U.N. flag has arrived to try and stabilize the country and help get the infrastructure up and going. Our job is to move burnt out cars and are directed to one particularly rural village where the only street is supposed to be blocked by a mountain of these things.

Only when we get there we can only find a couple of wrecks to be loaded and not much else seemed to be happening. "Must have the wrong place," my map reading side-kick says. "The village is supposed to be full of them."

At that point an old lady ventures over and starts pointing up a track: "Mini: Mini:" she says.

"Thank you," I reply, smiling down at her, and set off driving our recovery vehicle up the rutted track to collect the mini.

An old man is flagging us down: "Mini: Mini:" he says, pointing further up the track which is becoming narrower and greener by the minute.

"Thank you," I say, smiling down at him and moving off.

Another hundred yards; and another old chap is standing in the middle of the track; arms outstretched.

"Looks like we're here," my co-pilot says, jumping down.

"Mini: Mini:" shouts the man.

"Where-is-the-car," asks Jock?

"Mini: Mini:"

"Yes-mini: Where-is-the-mini?"

The man is waving his arms about now; really agitated: He's pointing everywhere.

Jock looks perplexed; thinking, 'Nutter.'

"Hang-on a second, Jock," I shout down? "I've got an English-Yugoslav dictionary here somewhere."   "Mini-mini-mini," I keep repeating to myself, as I flick the pages. "Err: Jock!"

"Yep!"

"Mini doesn't mean mini, as in a car."

"Well, what does it mean?"

"It means we're in the middle of a ****** mine-field."

Cyprus: Two hundred yards from the frontier with the northern side of the island and under the watchful eyes of the Turkish soldiers stationed on the front line.

Our mission: To drive dumper trucks, loaded with aggregate, from the quarry two miles away, down a dusty track, across a highway and deliver the load to the site of a new road.

A no-brainer: And with no problems, we soon get bored – and the time trials start. I hold the record: 2 minutes 27 seconds:

Only 'Pig' was determined to beat it. [He wanted to be called 'Beast,' but there was no way he'd get away with choosing his own nickname: So, Pig: And ten years later he was still, Pig.] The only way he could make up time on the record, was to take a chance: Accelerate the dumper as you went up the ramp to the highway; keep the throttle open – and hope.

Pig hits the ramp so fast that he takes off; flies the road without touching the tarmac; then nose-dives onto the dusty track on the far side. With the throttle still wide open, he roars off to the finish: Time: 2.12: A full fifteen seconds off my record.

But I appeal: Any damage to the dumpers and you must be disqualified: And the heavy landing has bent the steering rod.

Pig is disqualified – even though he was the only one ever to fly a dumper.

*

It may have been the damage to the dumper. Maybe the sergeant had been watching through his binoculars from the roof of his metal container-cum-office at the far side of the site. Who knows? But all the drivers were paraded in front of him for a mass bollocking. All except one that is: Pig. He had decided to go off in his dumper to get another load, or some more practice. Not that the sergeant had missed him - so far.

The telling off went well. We were driving too fast; we were driving dangerously; we were damaging vehicles; we were a disgrace; we were ....

The distinctive sound of a distant dumper came to our ears. The guts were being revved out of it. The sergeant paused momentarily, pulled a face and began, "You useless............" He stopped. The dumper was coming fast. Pig must be giving it some real wellie. The whining noise was overpowering, even the sergeant's cup was rattling and then window panes joined in.

"This is what I mean," he shouted, running to the door and snatching it open.

Pig went past at the speed of light, leaving the sergeant coughing and spluttering as a cloud of dust and gravel enveloped him.

It was hard, really hard, not to laugh.

IT ONLY TAKES A MINUTE

Northern Ireland: I'm newly arrived in the province and working with my Staff Sergeant. I really want to make a good impression, but you know what happens – the harder you try…..

We're operating a Minute-man; a mini-drill used for taking earth samples, and whereas it's heavy, the two of us were coping well enough.

"Can you manage for a couple of minutes," my sergeant asks?

You don't say 'no' in these circumstances, so off he goes. Only the drill isn't on totally level ground and slowly topples over. Not that I knew anything about it; until it crashed down on my head.

I'm out: Unconscious and bleeding. Ten seconds later, I'm wide awake. Burning oil is covering my clothes, my hands; my face: It's even running down my neck.

I'm up, looking all about me and hoping no one is watching. The last thing I need as the new boy is to give them something to laugh at. 'I'm okay,' I convince myself. 'Got to get cleaned up: I know: Head for the river.'

I kneel down. The water is two feet below the level of the bank. I lean forward: Plop! I must have still been befuddled – because I couldn't make out what that sound was: Plop!

I cleaned up as best I could and was heading back to the upturned Minute-man, when I realized what the sound was: Plop!

I check my holster under the leather jacket: The revolver isn't there any more: It's in the river.

I run back: Up to the waist in the water; trawling for the weapon. I find it; charge back to the machinery; with super-human strength, I get it back upright before the sergeant returns.

I couldn't tell him: In the two minutes he'd left me alone, I'd knocked myself unconscious; broken the Minute-man; been burned by oil – and lost my weapon. But I had to think on my feet to explain why I was soaking wet through…..

THE INVISIBLE MAN

We're in civilian clothes working along the border with Eire. Our job was to survey the route of a new road, marking it out by sticking poles in the ground. It was tedious work; boring – so we enliven the day by chucking stuff at one another; kicking a football about: All good natured fun.

I head off over a fence to get the ball back.

'Oooh:' Ever such a tiny, low groan.

"What's that," I shout back to my mate?

"I didn't say nuthin'," he replies.

"Firk off:" A tiny voice; hardly audible. Could it be one of these Irish leprechauns I'd heard so much about?

"Hello," I whisper in the direction of my feet; you know; real quiet as you don't want to frighten a fairy.

"Firk off, will ye."

I bend down to get the ball - and come eye-ball to eye-ball with the whites of the eyes of an S.A.S. bloke who was lost in the hedge bottom.

"I've spent two days watching that bloody terrorist's house over there and you've just cocked it up."

I retrieved the ball, unable to speak with embarrassment; and then unable to explain to my mate why I'd suddenly been consumed by the work ethic - sticking poles in as fast as possible and heading for our truck.

THE MAD DRUMMER

Great Falls, Montana: We'd booked into the motel for the night; washed and changed, then headed back to the reception for advice as to where to get a drink.

"There's a night club down the highway," the young lady drawls, "But it's about four miles away."

We pull a face: Couldn't take the car as we all needed a few beers. "Taxi," we ask?

"Don't bother, lads," said a rather large, be-suited gentleman with a Stetson. "I'll drop you off."

"Cheers mate."

"Anything to help our Limey cousins."

Once outside, our ride was a stretch-limo, complete with drinks cabinet, television; the works. A glimmer of an idea: "Would you mind opening the door for us when we get there, Jim?"

"Sure thing."

And that's what he did.

"Thank you, James," we say as we get out in front of a long line of would-be clubbers. "Three a.m. Don't be late."

"I won't, young sirs," Jim answers, acting for all he's worth.

You could hear the buzz going along the line: "These guys must be special," they were saying — an idea fostered by the actions of the bouncers on the door who ushered us in straight away.

Great!

Once inside, the word soon got around 'we' were there: A rock band or some such. The night club owner waddles over and we decide that we'd milk this for all it was worth: "Who are you guys?" he asks, in a real-friendly fashion.

"A rock group out from the U.K." says Geordie.

"On tour," the boss asks?

"Yeah: Got a few gigs lined up."

"What's the name of your group?"

We're getting to the hard questions now; but Geordie isn't fazed. He gives the name of a long defunct band he'd once played in back on his native Tyneside.

"I've heard of you, guys:" [Which was more than I had.] "Free drinks for these lads," he shouts to the bartender. "And keep 'em coming."

This was working out much better than we'd expected: A free lift to the club; straight in without queuing – and now free drinks.

Word got around the club: We're now a world famous group on tour – and so spend plenty of time signing autographs.

There's a live band playing that night – and they are pretty good, but come the interval when they take a ten minute break, we have a crisis.

The club owner is back. "Any chance of you doing a number on stage for us," he asks? "A bit of promo-work for my club: We'll take a picture of you and I'll hang it on the wall."

"Sure," says Geordie. He had nothing to worry about. Drunk or sober, he could play the drums as good as any professional that I'd ever heard.

"Sure," says Dicky. He can play the electric guitar.

That leaves Woody and me. We couldn't play a note on anything.

Woody gets in first: "Sorry," he says, and shows a bandage on his hand from an accident he'd had at work the previous week. "I'm rhythm guitar but….." The bandage does his talking for him.

All eyes are on me now, and I'm beginning to wish I was back in the motel emptying the mini-bar.

"I'm the singer," I lied. "I'm afraid I'm not allowed to perform anywhere other than at the approved venues. It's all legal stuff…..If I lose my voice and the tour has to be curtailed….."

"I understand completely," says the club owner; no doubt seeing lawyers queuing up to take him for millions.

"Come on, Dicky," says Geordie, distracting the owner from my red face: [It always goes red when I tell porky-pies.] And off they went on stage to join a couple of the professional band members.

The club's going wild because the two 'super-stars' are doing their stuff; not that there was much special going on – for starters: All nice, easy listening.

Then it came to the drum solo – and Geordie went berserk: "Look at him go!" People were crammed in the aisles; pressed up against the stage. It was a marvellous performance. Their drummer sidles over: "Does he know what he's doin?" he asks.

"Sure," I replied, trying to allay the concerns he was starting to have over the safety of his expensive kit. "He's a pro." I turn away cringing as Geordie hit the drums harder and harder.

End of the night: We're carried out on a tide of cheering and a stamping of feet; enough to bring the house down.

Only there was no limousine waiting. Dare we sneak back in and phone for a taxi?

Bosnia: A convoy of Royal Engineers' vehicles are winding their weary way through a narrow mountain pass; a wall of rock to one side of the road; a drop of several hundred feet on the other. But unlike most road edges in this part of the world, this wasn't a vertical drop, the land slipped away at a gentle 45 degree angle.

In the convoy was an AVRE; [Armoured Vehicle Royal Engineers,] basically an old Chieftain tank with its gun removed and piled high with engineering equipment.

The vehicles rumble along the mountainside; the road going up and down interminably; and then, on one of the down slopes, the gear box of the tank gives up the ghost. And if there is no gear box; there's no brakes. And on a road with many bends and long drops, it doesn't take a genius to abandon ship: The tank crew jump for their lives – no time for niceties like switching the engine off.

The Chieftain picks up speed and goes over the precipice.

"Couldn't have picked a better place," says the sergeant, as the tank rumbles and speeds its way down the 45 degree embankment. "Anywhere else and….." The sergeant stopped mid-sentence to watch fascinated as the vehicle reaches the valley floor; girds itself, fords the river and is up and out into the small trees on the far side.

The trees are simply devoured by the monster; knocked flat – but the explosions as they hit the ground were somewhat unexpected. Was it the tank engine blowing up? But no: Three explosions later, the tank is out into a meadow and still going.

"Couldn't have picked a better place," the sergeant continues: "Should be a doddle to recover it from there." Only he's no longer looking at the tank, but at the map he's got stretched out on the Land Rover bonnet.

BOOM…..BOOM! Columns of fire and dirt streak upwards; pieces of the tank tracks join them. But at least it had stopped.

"You could-a picked a better place, lads," said the sergeant nonchalantly, having changed his mind. "It's in the middle of a bloody minefield."

It took days to get it back.

The order of the day: Everyone – but everyone – will wear a red nose.

The S.S.M. is a great supporter of whatever charity is the flavour of the month: Kids' toys for Christmas; food for Africa: Red Nose Day for Comic Relief. He'd support anything; only today it was Red Nose day – and if you don't wear one, the punishment was two hours drill in double-time around the parade square.

We're given permission to go and buy a nose: "Twenty minutes: No more." And that was okay. Although the NAAFI canteen selling them was on the neighbouring army camp, we could be there and back easily in fifteen.

Only things didn't go according to plan:

Four of us buy the noses and put them on, marching out of the shop and heading back

to our own regimental camp. We'd only gone some twenty yards when this unintelligible screaming could be heard in the distance.

"Someone's copping it," I volunteered.

"Good job it's nothing to do with us," says Jock who was marching next to me.

The screaming continues for a while – we ignore it – and it stops. We approach the front gate of our sister regiment, only to be met at the barrier by the Provo sergeant, complete with a red face and a shout to match. "What do you think….." he's screaming at us.

It would appear that a R.S.M. had seen our noses and had gone ballistic. As we'd ignored his screams, he'd taken it out on the Provo by screaming at him down the phone. Hence the Provo's red face.

The R.P. wouldn't allow us to speak – just started the punishment as directed by the R.S.M. there and then: Two hours drill in double-time around his parade square.

It was a long two hours before we were allowed to march back to our own camp, drenched in sweat and with very red faces instead of red noses.

We made it to the camp gates – only to be met by a R.P. sergeant who had a very red face courtesy of our own S.S.M. who'd gone ballistic at him for us going missing. The message: "Skiving were we? Well, we were going to be made to suffer."

Fortunately, our Provo sergeant was a little more reasonable than the previous one and allowed us to go and present ourselves to the S.S.M. rather than showing us where the drill square was.

Now, red noses in place and a perfect match for our red faces, we march into his presence. He hears us out; his face getting redder and redder and redder. He's on the phone really blasting the R.P. sergeant at the other camp. We almost felt sorry for him as, no doubt, his face was getting redder and redder – again.

We were asked to leave before our S.S.M. spoke to his opposite number in the camp next door; but I would think there'd be red-faced temper-tantrums going on behind closed doors.

I often wonder if the celebrities on the telly – the ones counting the cash being pledged, ever know just how much red-faced sweaty-effort goes into earning a few quid for them.

READY, AIM…….?

Did you ever wonder what goes on in the mind of a Coldstream Guardsman on duty outside Buckingham Palace? They stand like statues for what seems an age, letting tourists take all sorts of liberties.

However, the guardsmen are allowed to move every twenty minutes or so to relieve the monotony and get the blood circulating. To make this fifty metre trip worth while, the game is to wait until a tourist – usually a Japanese tourist who is festooned with cameras and lenses and tripods – to set up all the equipment; [and it can take a long time, measuring exposures and the like,] then move just before the photograph is taken.

March the fifty metres; come to attention – and wait. The tourist is soon lugging all the equipment along to the new position; setting it up – and…..the guardsman moves back.

It helps pass the time.

CHINESE WHISPERS

I suppose everyone knows of the message sent along the front line trenches of the 1st World War: "Send reinforcements. We're going to advance."

By the time it reached the General at headquarters, the message read: "Send three and four pence: We're going to a dance."

I'm assured it's true: And so is this one:

In battle code, [BATCO;] the officer in command of clearance and reconstruction operations deep in Bosnia, flashes a message back to his headquarters: "Send a quarry excavator to grid reference….."

The message caused some consternation when it was received – yet with commendable speed things were organized. The Commanding Officer 'out there' must get what he wants – and now. Two men are immediately despatched to the other side of the country to ensure the safe arrival of…..a coffee percolator.

THE WEST-SIDE IMP

West Belfast at the height of 'The Troubles' is probably as good a place as any to bring this epistle to a close. Each soldier is said to have 'his war:' For some it was the Falklands, Iraq, Afghanistan or any number of places anywhere across the globe: But for me it was the 'Dirty War' of Northern Ireland.

*

Another day: Another protest. Only this time the residents of West Belfast decide to block the main road into the city by parking their own cars across the highway.

The cops and security forces turn up and negotiations begin. Only tensions and tempers are running high. The result: "We shall not, we shall not be moved:" The chief spokesmen begins to sing and his supporters immediately join in: "We shall not….."

The road block is for staying put; that much was obvious to the police inspector. He asks nicely: "Please….."

"No chance: We shall not, we shall not be moved:" Another chorus.

"Pretty please."

"Go * yersell."

"I'll have to get the army to remove your cars one by one," the policeman reasons.

"Okay," the negotiator agrees. "You do that; it'll save face. Only don't scratch my car: It's that little Hillman Imp over there."

That ensured the tiny car became first choice for the army vehicle fitted with a rusty grab. It trundled forward following the policeman's pointing and waving.

"Don't scratch it, mind," says the spokesman looking more than a little worried by now. "It's nearly a classic and….."

The steel grab begins to open its jaws as it's lowered toward the Imp: Its huge teeth look somewhat uncompromising: Unyielding in the face of the protester's screams: "Don't scratch it!"

His screams are drowned-out by the noise of the grab smashing down onto the metal roof: The windows explode; glass everywhere. Then the car is up and swinging high in the air, before being dropped in two pieces onto the back of a waiting lorry.

"Next!" shouts the army grab-operator, no doubt enjoying himself immensely. But he's too late. The dash to remove the road block was remarkable; completed within seconds accompanied by the revving of engines, screeching of tyres and a pall of blue smoke.

The now-Impless negotiator was left alone on the near deserted street; sick at heart and no doubt cursing his choice of defiant, song of protest.

"We sha-all, we shall be moved….." sang the squaddie driver.

"We sha-all, we shall be moved….." joined in the police choir.

Off the disconsolate negotiator trudged, his shoulders hunched forlornly, head bowed. He was so inconsolable that he even missed his golden opportunity, when asked, "Where shall I put your car?"

July, 2003: My time is up in the army: Not that I want to leave; I'd enjoyed my seventeen years. Yet, to some extent, I reckon I can share the same experience - of leaving the familiar — with one of my great grandfathers; John Ryan, who'd fought in the Peninsula War against Napoleon. John was ten years older than me when he was invalided out; his discharge papers read: *'Old, worn out and lame.'* Well; one out of the three was the same.

August, 2003: Civvy Street — and a million miles from my former life. Time for a decision: One thing was for certain: I'm not going to take the job on offer in the factory — or any factory, for that matter. I've just watched a bloke feed a metal rod into a machine; one every eight seconds — for hours on end. It makes me realize what I've had to leave behind - and I'm so thankful for my life in the army that there's a lump in my throat. I feel I should go and tell the metal worker that there is another life 'out there:' 'Join up!'

But I don't. It's not my place — and anyway, the Army he'd experience would be totally different from the one I'd joined: Or indeed the one Granddad Ryan had joined. I can only speak for my time: We worked hard; then played hard. Weeks of full-on work, followed by the rewards: Courses and qualifications in skiing, parachuting, basketball, rugby: You name it and it was available.

By the time I was discharged, operational duties ruled: Tour followed tour, relentlessly: Too many commitments: Not enough men: Not enough equipment: Too little time for family. The balance had gone.

Yet, I wonder if this is so different from times gone by: Did they have enough men or equipment; did you get time with the family during Napoleonic times; or in the trenches of the First World War; or in the jungles of the Far East during the 1940's? Probably not: But in this day and age, when the scenes of war are in your living room every day of the week; the young, future recruits are going to have to be convinced that a career in the armed forces is right for them: They will need substantial 'carrots;' substantial assurances as to their futures - or governments will be unable to avoid conscription.

Yet, behind the politics, I believe all soldiers, throughout the ages, have had the same mind-set.

As the Duke of Wellington once remarked of his troops:
They were always; *"Guessing at what was on the other side of the hill."*

It's what sets us apart.

Some Abbreviations:

A.V.R.E.	Armoured vehicle; Royal Engineers
Basher	Make shift tent
Bergen	Rucksack
B.F.T.	Basic Fitness Test
C.O	Commanding Officer – Usually a Colonel
C.S.B.	Combat support boat
Dessy Wellies	Civilian, sand coloured, suede ankle boots.
Full screw	Corporal
G.P.M.G	General Purpose Machine Gun
Harbour area	An army campsite.
I.V.C.P	Illegal Vehicle Check Point.
Jack	Someone being selfish, thoughtless, etc.
Lance jack	Lance Corporal
Maggot	A sleeping bag
M.G.B.	Medium Girder Bridge
NAAFI	Navy, Army and Air Force Institute
N.B.C.	Nuclear Biological Chemical
N.C.O.	Non-commissioned officer
Noddy Kit	N.B.C suit
O.C	Officer Commanding – Usually a Major
O.P	Observation Point/Post
Provo	Usually a Sergeant with attitude in charge of guardroom
Provo's	Terrorists
QMSI	Warrant Officer in charge of stores
Razzman	Regimental Sergeant Major
Rupert	Officer

R.P.	Regimental Police
R&R.	Rest and recuperation
R.S.M.	Regimental Sergeant Major
Scammell:	A big truck: [A very big truck.]
S.L.R.	Self Loading Rifle.
S.M.G.	Sub machine gun
S.S.M.	Squadron Sergeant Major
Sprog	Soldier just out of training
Staffy	Staff Sergeant
Stag/Stag on	Sentry duty
Stickman.	Squadron Sergeant Major

Other titles by Ian Patterson:

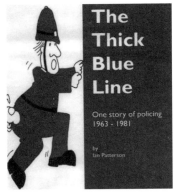

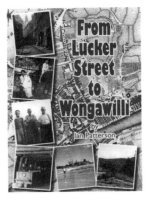

Hilarious police stories from the 1960's and 1970's; with line drawings by John Patterson.

Charting the emigration of families from industrial Tyneside to Australia over 200 years. Amusing anecdotes from the places they settled.

A new series of tour guides - 'SECRET SHREWSBURY'
Each of the four books takes you on a stroll around the centre of this remarkable and historic town. Through Ian's own brand of storytelling you will be amazed and entertained, but also you will see some of the hidden features within this loop of the River Severn

Available from GET Publishing www.getpublishingshop.co.uk